budgetbooks

ROCK GUITAR CLASSICS

ISBN 978-1-4234-9313-6

HAL•LEONARD®
CORPORATION
7777 W. BLUEMOUND RD. P.O. BOX 13819 MILWAUKEE, WI 53213

Visit Hal Leonard Online at
www.halleonard.com

CONTENTS

American Girl

Words and Music by Tom Petty

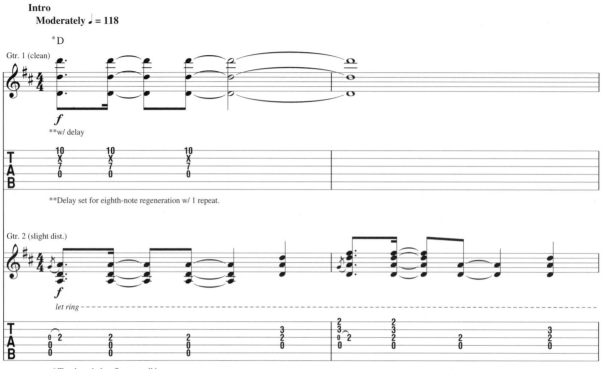

*Chord symbols reflect overall harmony.

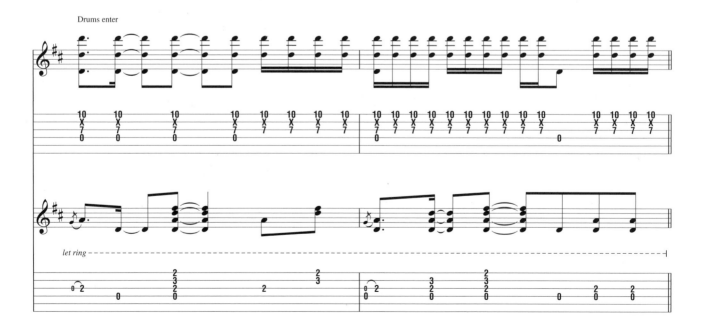

some - where _ else. _   Af - ter all it was a great big _ world _
waves   crash-in'on the beach. _   And for one des - per - ate _ mo - ment _ there, _

with lots of plac - es _ to run to. _   Yeah, and if _ she had to die
he crept _ back in her mem - o-ry. _   God, it's _ so pain - ful when

6

try - in' she
some-thin' that is so close

had one lit-tle prom-ise she was gon - na keep.
is still so far out of reach.

(Ah.

Chorus

G5   A5   D

Oh yeah,   al - right.   Take it eas - y, ba - by,

Ah.)

*Gtrs. 1 & 2

*Composite arrangement

Bm   G5   A5

make it last all night.   She was   an A - mer - i - can girl.
(Make it last all night.)

Outro-Guitar Solo

Bkgd. Voc.: w/ Voc. Fig. 1 (till fade)

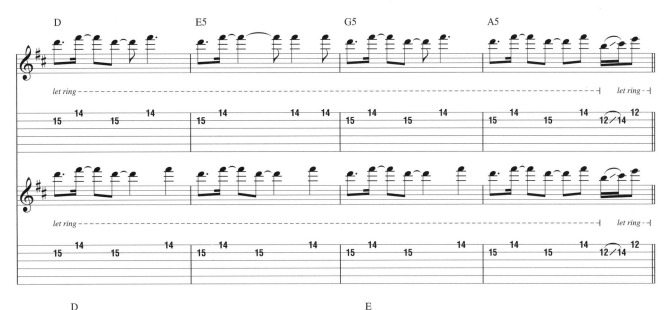

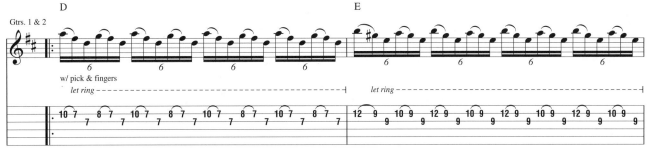

Repeat and fade

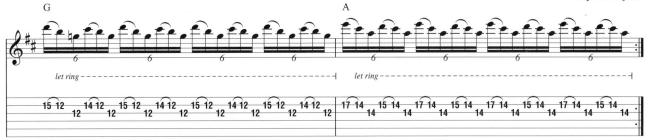

Authority Song

Words and Music by John Mellencamp

Double drop D tuning:
(low to high) D–A–D–G–B–D

Intro

Moderately fast Rock ♩ = 157

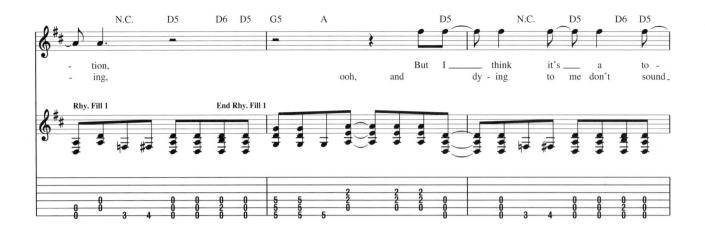

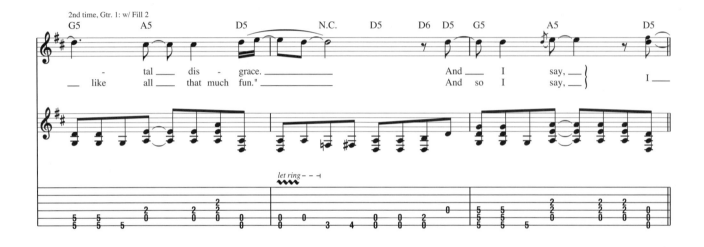

Chorus

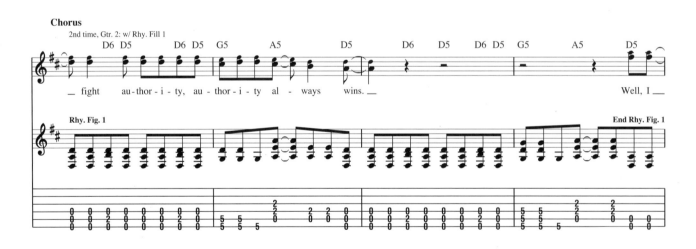

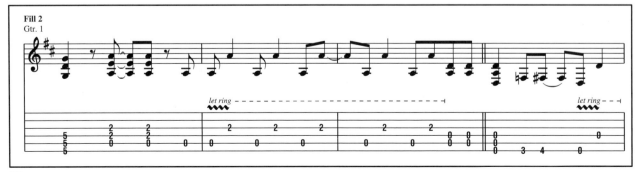

Guitar Solo

Gtrs. 1 & 2: w/ Rhy. Fig. 1 (4 times)

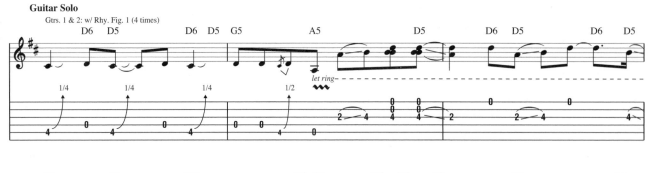

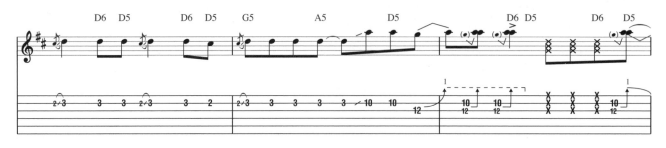

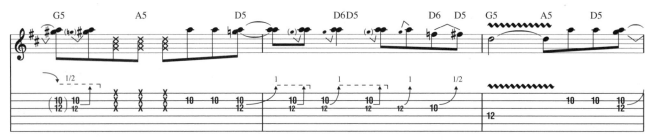

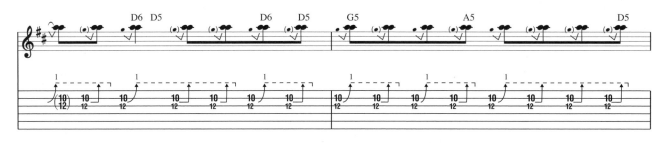

I say oh, _____

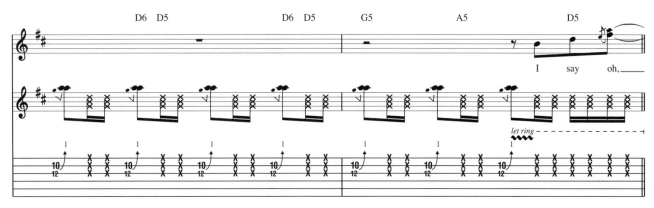

14

Burning for You

Words and Music by Donald Roeser and Richard Meltzer

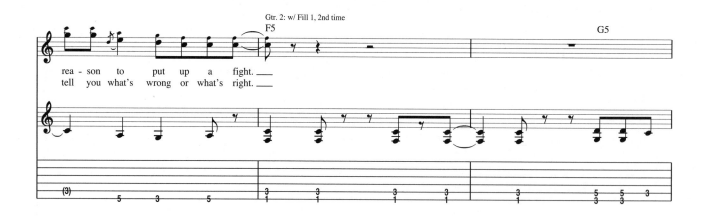

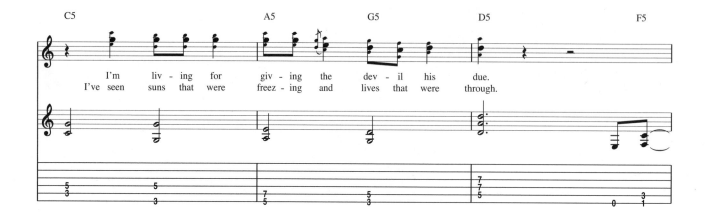

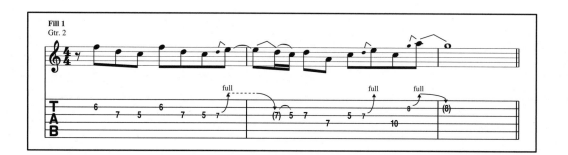

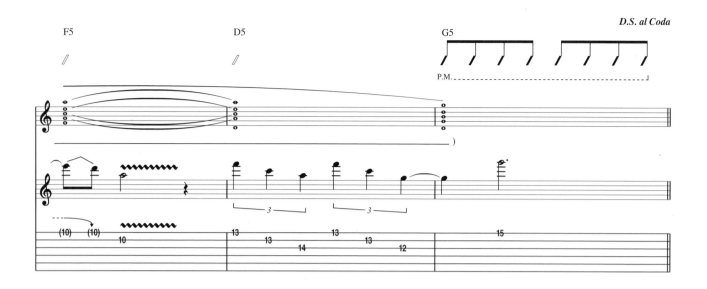

⊕ *Coda*

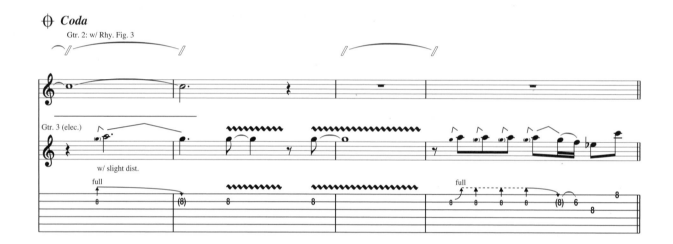

Guitar Solo

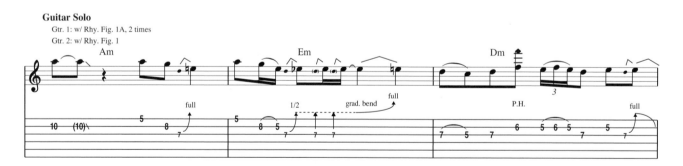

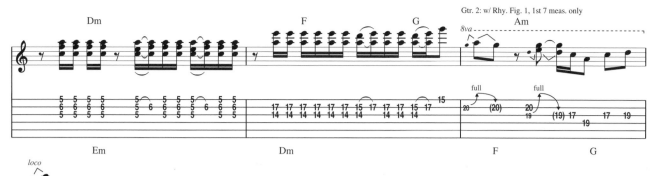

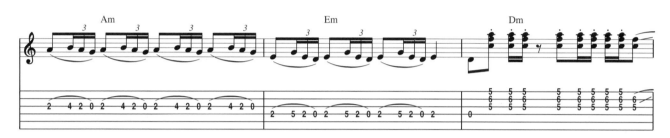

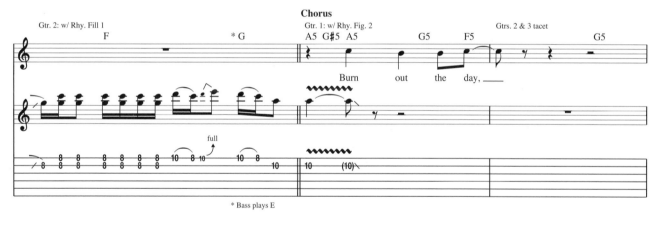

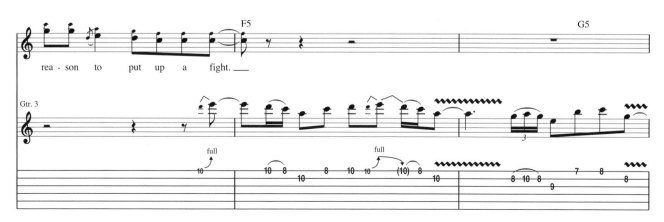

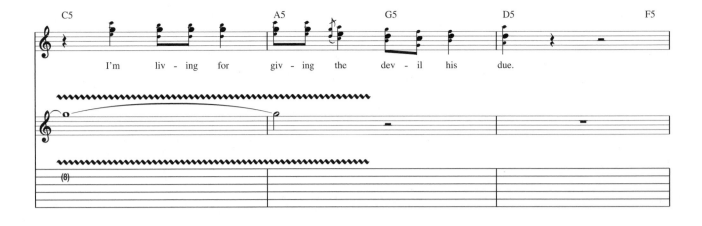

I'm liv-ing for giv-ing the dev-il his due.

And I'm burn-in', I'm ___ burn-in', I'm burn-in' for you. ___

Gtr. 1: w/ Rhy. Fig. 2, 1st 2 meas. only, 4 times

I'm burn-in', I'm ___

Gtr. 3

full   full   1/2

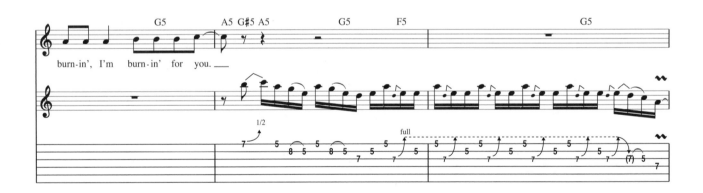

burn-in', I'm burn-in' for you. ___

1/2   full

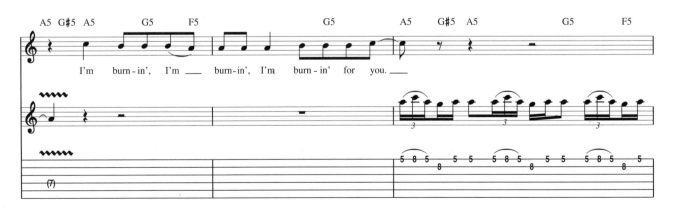

I'm burn-in', I'm ___ burn-in', I'm burn-in' for you. ___

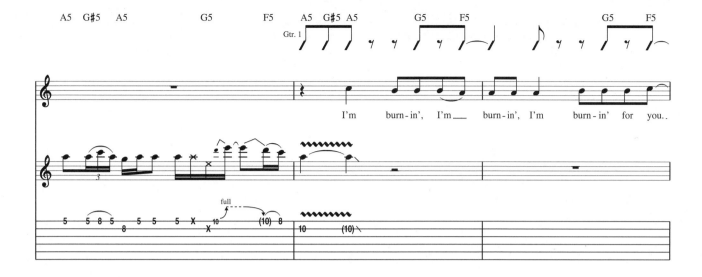

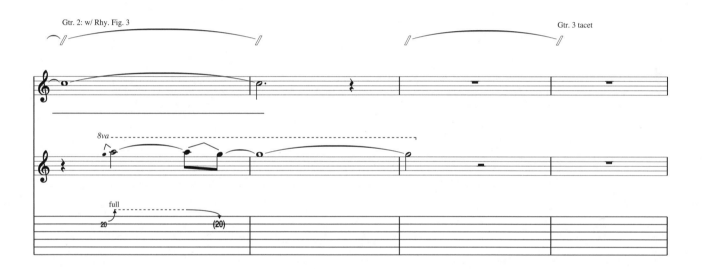

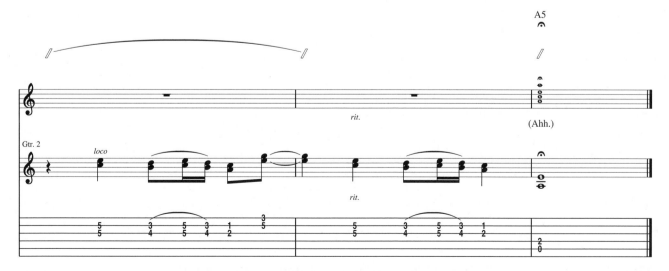

Cause We've Ended as Lovers

Words and Music by Stevie Wonder

*Chord symbols reflect overall harmony.

**Vol. swell

***Set for eighth-note regeneration w/ 1 repeat.

†Push down on string behind nut.

††Played w/ ring finger.

*Hammer onto note while manipulating vol. knob.

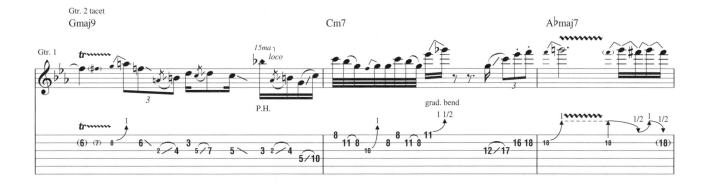

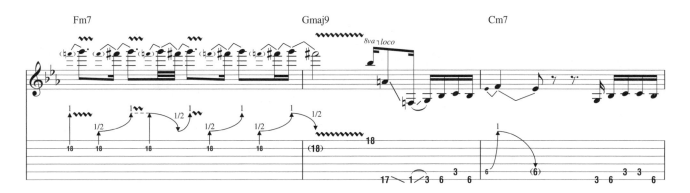

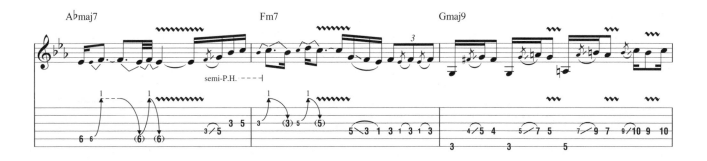

*Both strings caught and bent w/ ring finger.   **Played behind the beat.

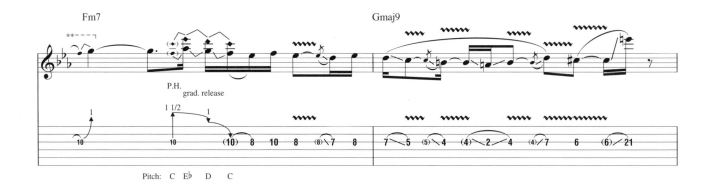

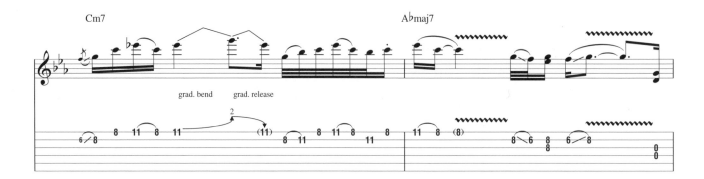

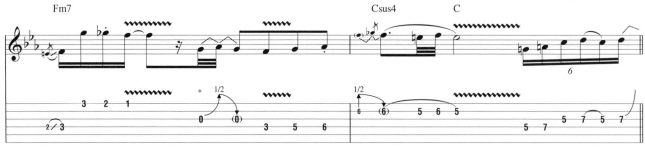

*Behind nut

32

I

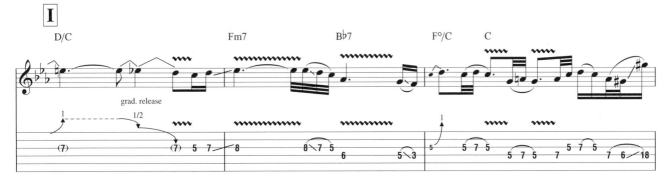

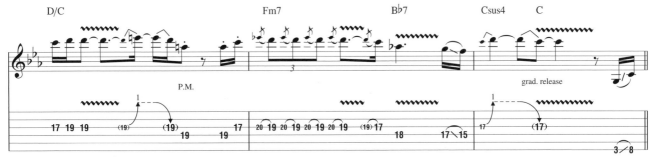

J

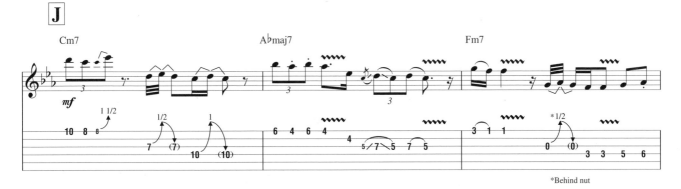

*Behind nut

K

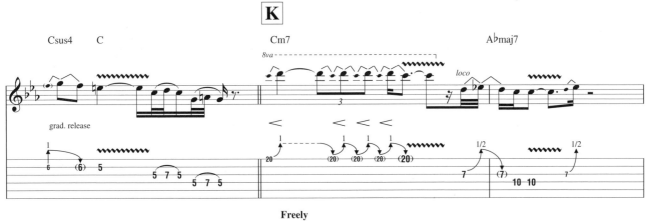

Freely

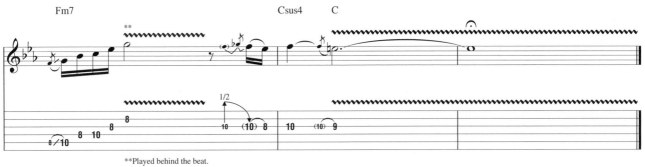

**Played behind the beat.

C'mon and Love Me

Words and Music by Paul Stanley

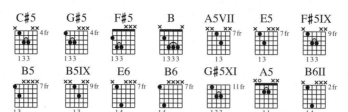

End Rhy. Fig. 2

Outro

Gtr. 1: w/Rhy. Fig. 3, 2 times

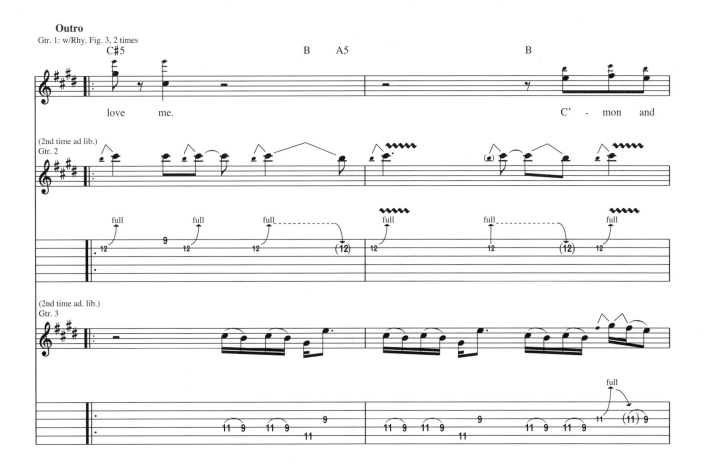

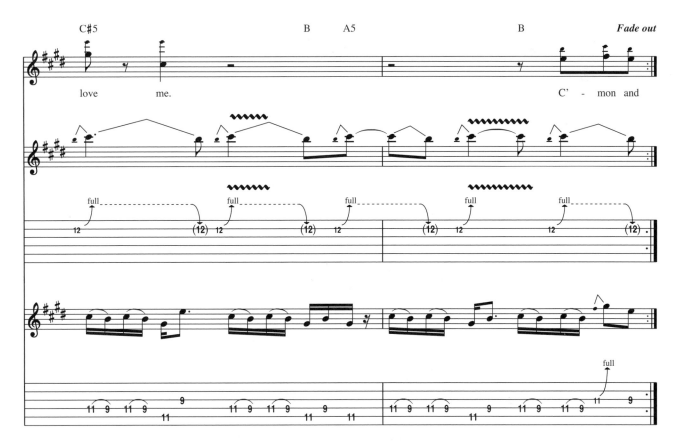

Dance the Night Away

Words and Music by David Lee Roth, Edward Van Halen, Alex Van Halen and Michael Anthony

*Chord symbols reflect basic harmony.

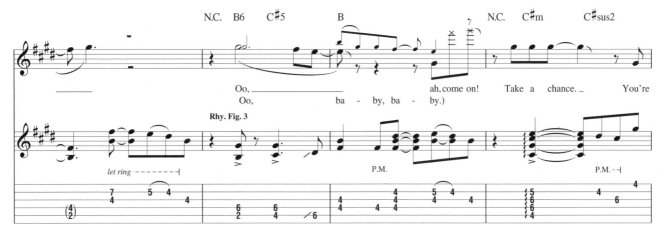

39

*Artificial harmonics produced by tapping strings 12 frets above fretted notes.

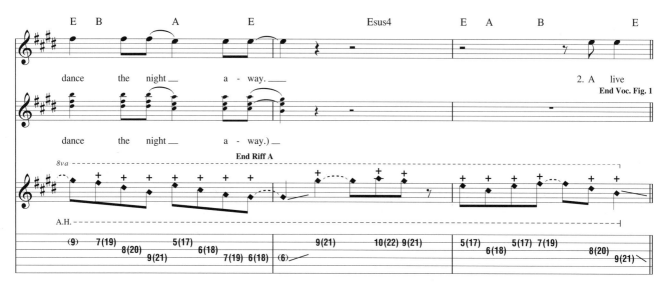

Verse

Gtr. 1: w/ Rhy. Fig. 2   Gtr. 2 tacet

wire, ___ bare - ly a be - gin - ner, but just watch that la - dy go. ___ She's on

fire ___ 'cause danc - in' gets her high - er than, uh, an - y - thing else she knows. ___

Gtr. 1

Pre-Chorus

N.C. B6 C#5   B   C#5   B

Oo, ___ won't ya turn your head my ___ way? ___
(Oo, ba - by, ba - by.

Gtr. 1: w/ Rhy. Fig. 3

N.C. B6 C#5   B   C#m C#sus2   B E B E

Oo, ___ Well, don't skip ro - mance _ 'cause you're old e - nough to dance _
Oo, ba - by, ba - by.)

Chorus

Bkgd. Voc: w/ Voc. Fig. 1
Gtr. 1: w/ Rhy. Fig. 1 (1st 6 meas.)
Gtr. 2: w/ Riff A

*Bass plays B.

Bridge

42

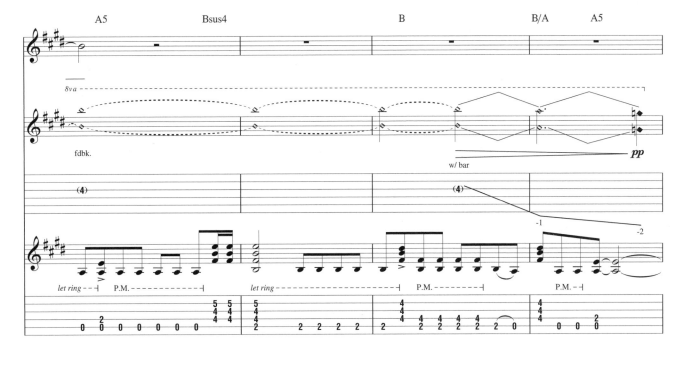

Interlude

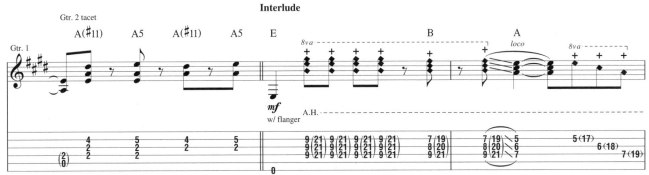

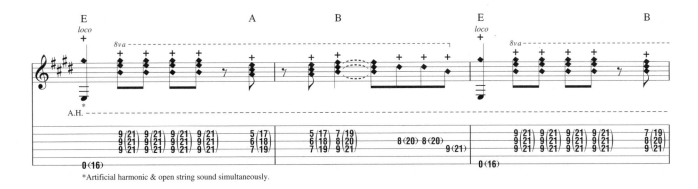

*Artificial harmonic & open string sound simultaneously.

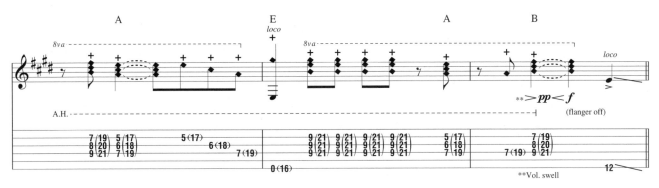

**Vol. swell

Outro-Chorus

Gtr. 1: w/ Rhy. Fig. 1
Gtr. 2: w/ Riff A (1st 4 meas.)

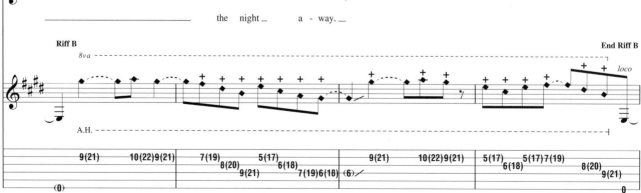

44

Gtr. 2: w/ Riff B (till fade)

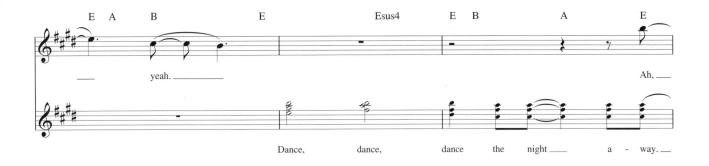

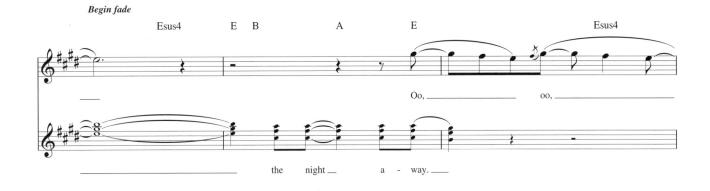

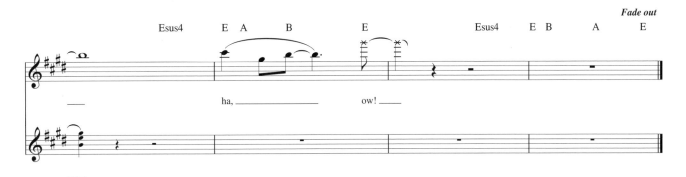

Don't Bring Me Down

Words and Music by Jeff Lynne

*Chord symbols reflect overall harmony.

1. You got me run-ning, go-ing out of my mind. You got me think-ing that I'm wast-ing my time. Don't bring me down. No, no, no, no, no. Oo, ee, hoo. I'll tell you once more be-fore I

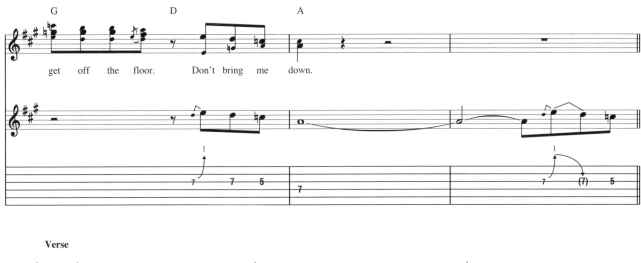

Verse

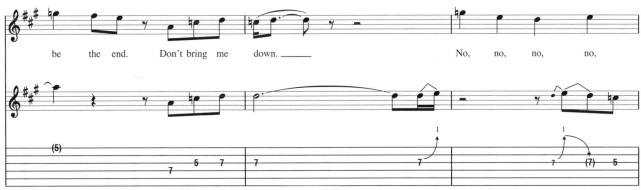

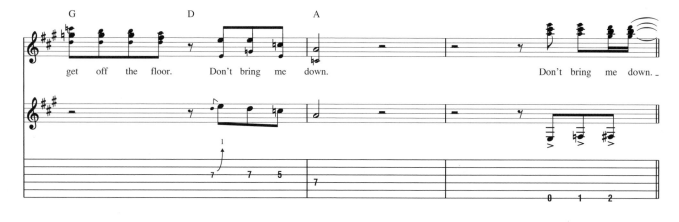

get off the floor. Don't bring me down.   Don't bring me down. _

Chorus

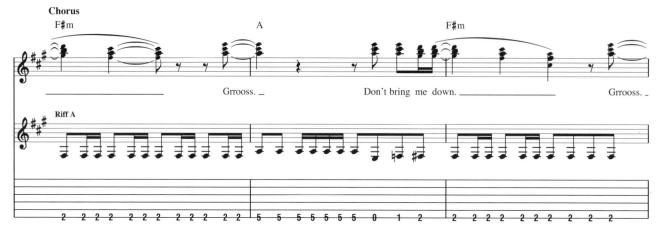

Grrooss. _   Don't bring me down. _   Grrooss. _

Riff A

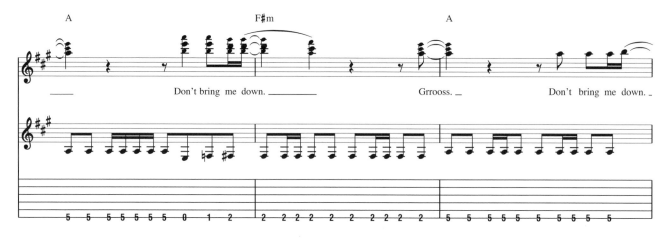

_ Don't bring me down. _____   Grrooss. _   Don't bring me down. _

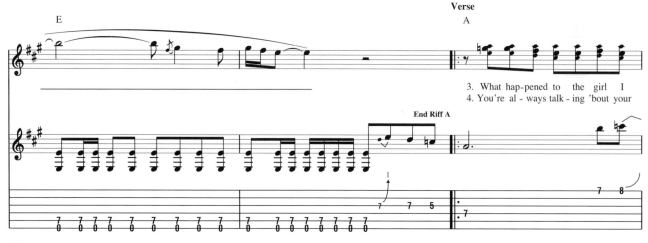

3. What hap-pened to the girl I
4. You're al-ways talk-ing 'bout your

End Riff A

used to know?   You let your mind out some-where down the road.   Don't bring me
cra - zy nights.   One of these days your gon-na get it right.

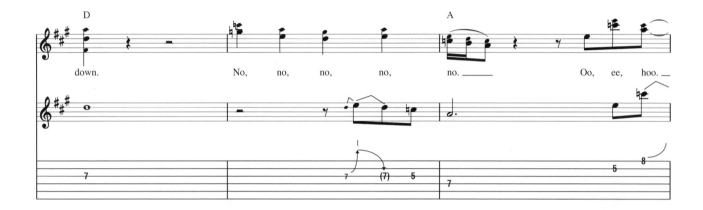

down.   No,   no,   no,   no,   no. _____   Oo, ee, hoo. __

I'll tell you once more be - fore I get off the floor.   Don't bring me

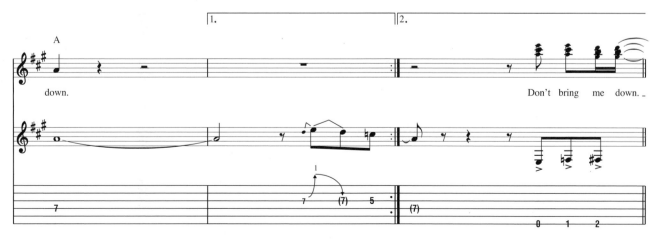

1.

2.

down.   Don't bring me down. _

49

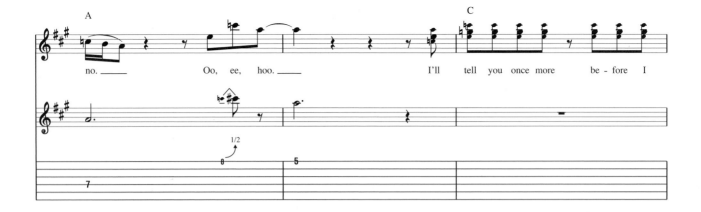

no. _____ Oo, ee, hoo. _____ I'll tell you once more be-fore I

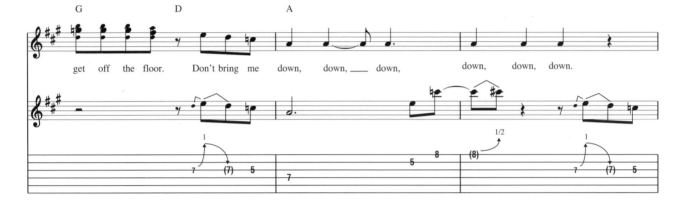

get off the floor. Don't bring me down, down, _____ down, down, down, down.

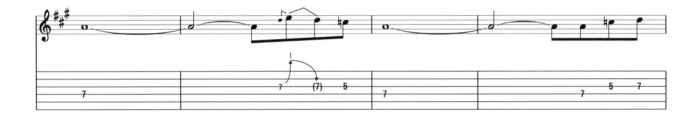

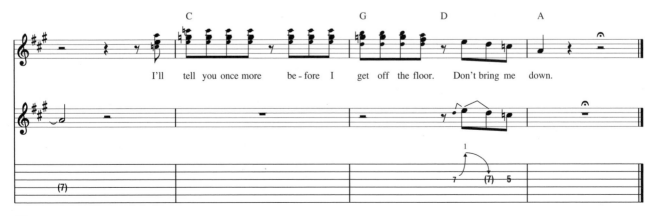

I'll tell you once more be-fore I get off the floor. Don't bring me down.

Down on the Corner

Words and Music by John Fogerty

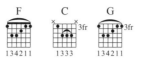

Intro
Medium Rock ♩ = 100

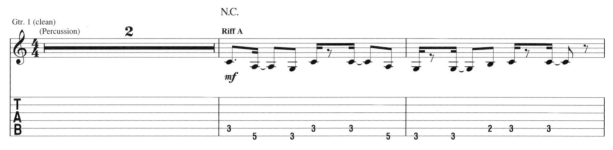

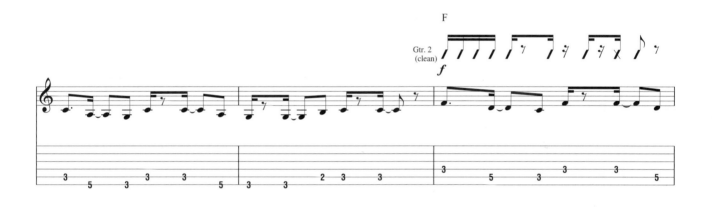

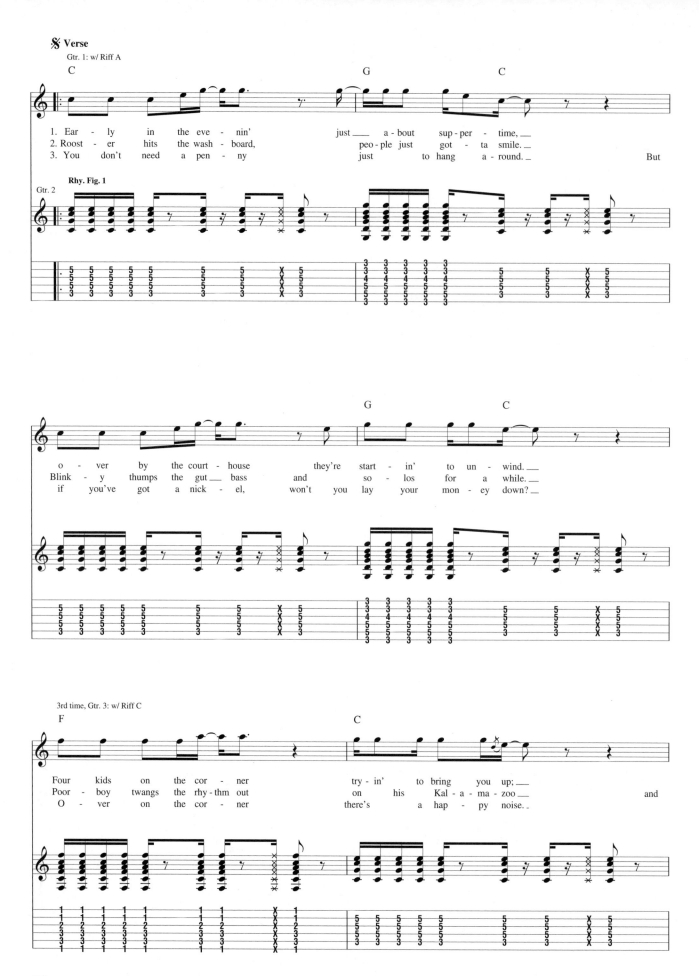

Interlude

Gtr. 1: w/ Riff A
Gtr. 2: w/ Rhy. Fig. 1

Gtr. 3 (clean)

Chorus

Gtr. 1: w/ Riff B
Gtr. 2: w/ Rhy. Fig. 2
Gtr. 3 tacet

Down on the cor - ner, out here in the street, ___ Wil - ly and the

Poor - boys are play - in'. Bring a nick - el, tap your feet. ___

Interlude

Gtr. 2: w/ Rhy. Fig. 1 (1st 4 meas.)

D.S. al Coda

Coda

Outro-Chorus

Gtr. 1: w/ Riff B (till fade)
Gtr. 2: w/ Rhy. Fig. 2 (till fade)

Down on the cor - ner, out here in the street, _ Wil - ly and the

Repeat & fade

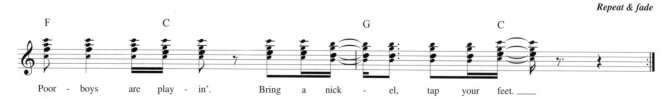

Poor - boys are play - in'. Bring a nick - el, tap your feet. ___

867-5309/Jenny

Words and Music by Alex Call and James Keller

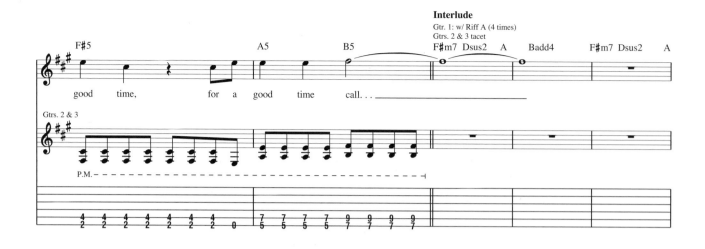

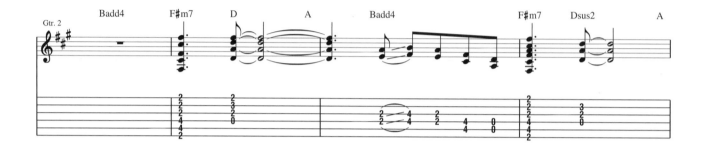

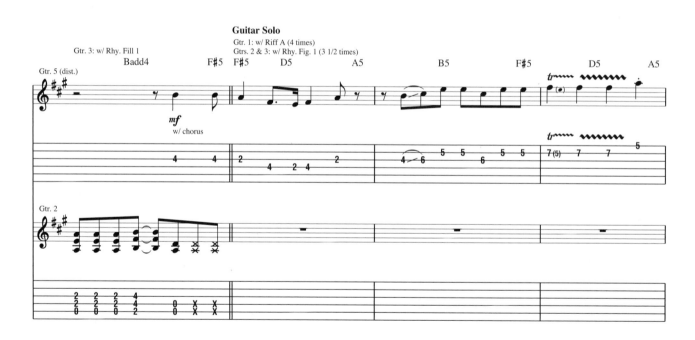

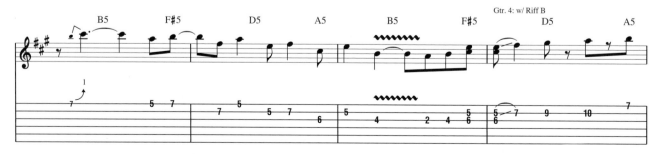

Fame

Words and Music by John Lennon, David Bowie and Carlos Alomar

just a flame___ that burns your change to keep you in   -   sane.___
just his line___ to bind your time, it drives you to   crime.___

1. sane. ___
2. crime. ___

Fame. ___
Fame. ___
Fame. ___)

Coda

Verse

Gtr. 3: w/ Rhy. Fig. 1, 4 times
Gtr. 2: w/ Riff B, 3 1/2 times
Gtr. 5: w/ Rhy. Fig. 2, simile

3. Is it an-y won-der, I re-ject you first? Fame, fame, fame,

fame. Is it an-y won-der, you are too cool to fool?

Fire and Water

Words and Music by Paul Rodgers and Andy Fraser

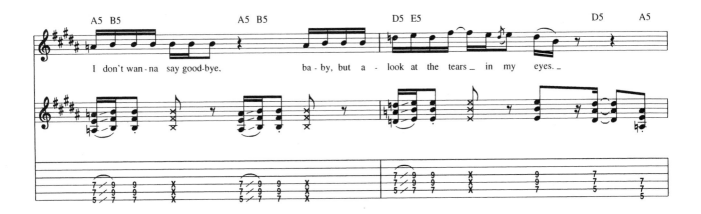

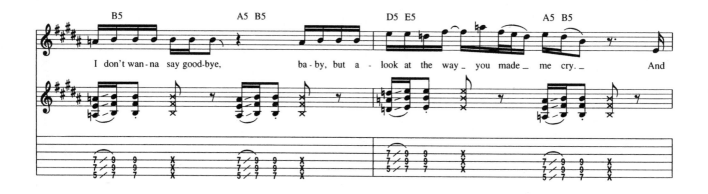

I don't wan-na say good-bye, ba-by, but a- look at the way you made me cry. And

ev-er-y-where is nice, huh. You show you got a heart that's made of ice. And I know

Chorus

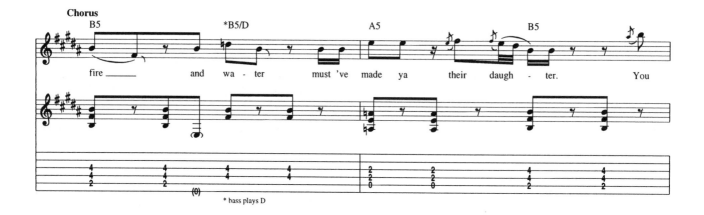

fire ___ and wa-ter must've made ya their daugh-ter. You

* bass plays D

got what it takes to make a poor man's heart break.

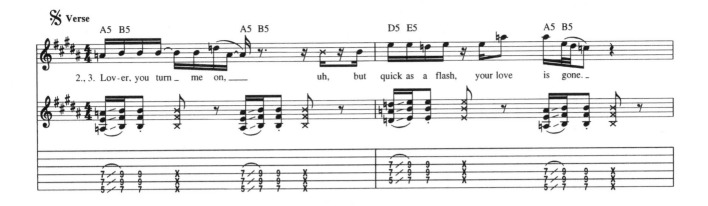

2., 3. Lov-er, you turn __ me on, ____ uh, but quick as a flash, your love is gone. __

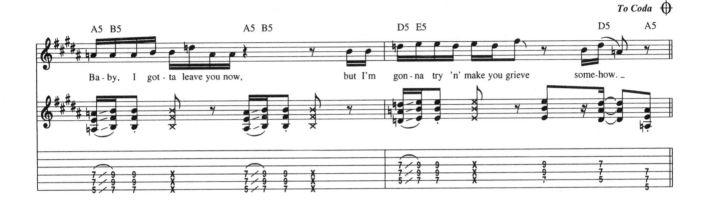

To Coda ⊕

Ba - by, I got - ta leave you now, but I'm gon - na try 'n' make you grieve some-how. __

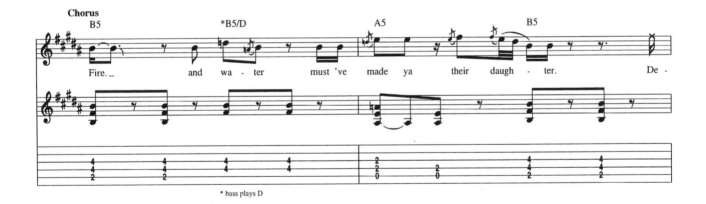

Chorus

Fire. __ and wa - ter must 've made ya their daugh - ter. De -

* bass plays D

praved, you got what it takes to make this old __ heart of mine break. ____

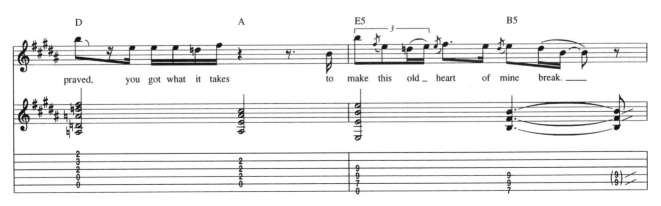

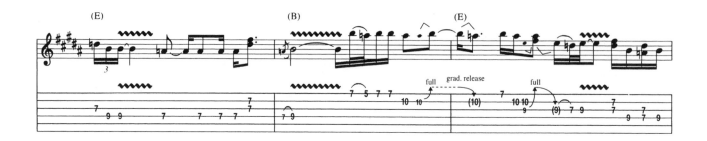

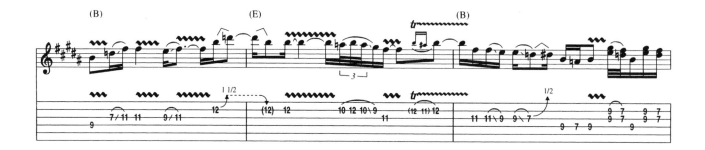

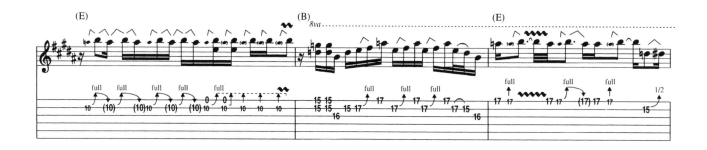

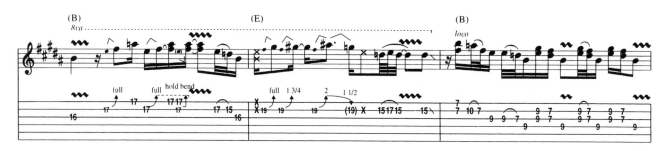

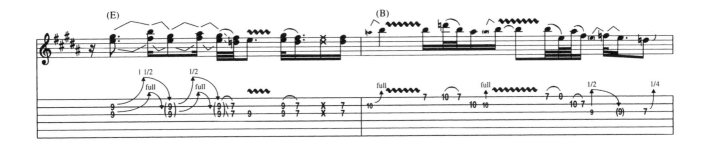

D.S. al Coda

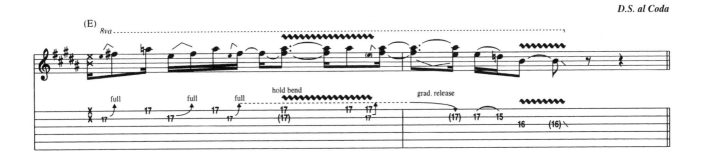

Coda

Chorus

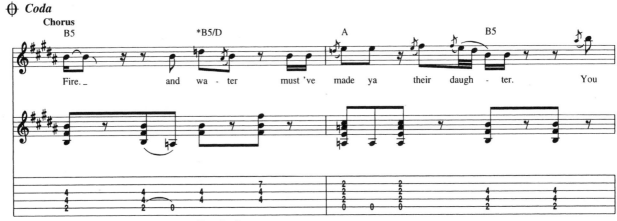

Fire. _ and wa-ter must've made ya their daugh-ter. You

* bass plays D

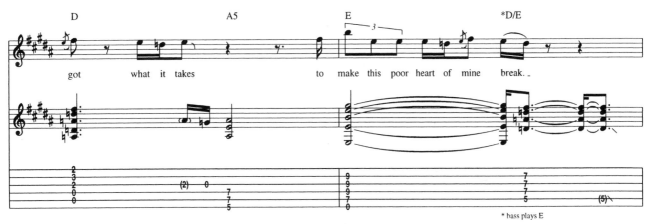

got what it takes to make this poor heart of mine break. _

* bass plays E

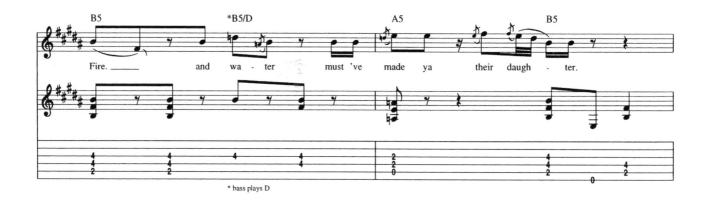

Fire. _____ and wa - ter must 've made ya their daugh - ter.

* bass plays D

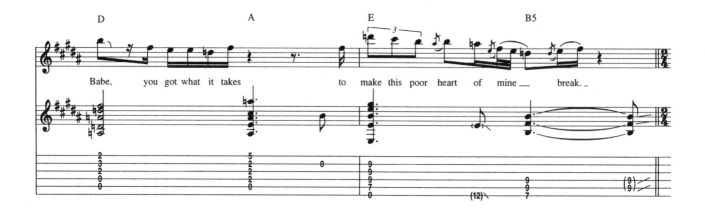

Babe, you got what it takes to make this poor heart of mine _____ break. __

Outro

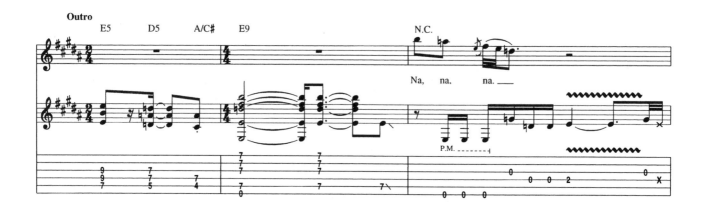

Na, na, na. _____

P.M. ----------

w/ Voc. ad Libs. till end

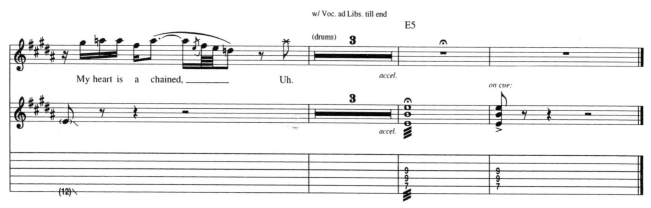

My heart is a chained, _____ Uh.

(drums)

accel.

on cue:

accel.

Glamour Boys

Words and Music by Vernon Reid

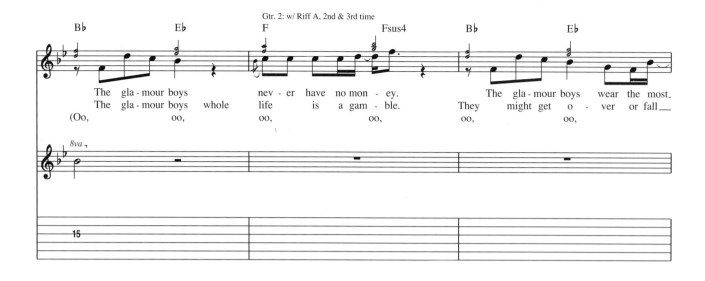

The gla-mour boys never have no mon-ey.
The gla-mour boys whole life is a gam-ble.
(Oo, oo, oo, oo,
The gla-mour boys wear the most_
They might get o - ver or fall__
oo, oo,

___ ex - pen - sive clothes. ___
___ flat on __ their face. ___
oo,
The gla-mour boys are al - ways at the par - ty
But if one does, there's no need to wor - ry,
oo, oo, oo, oo.

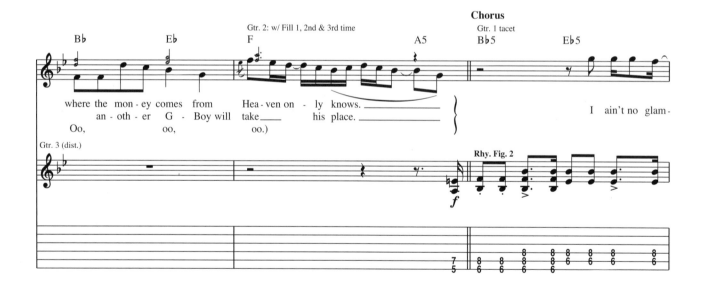

Chorus

where the mon - ey comes from Hea - ven on - ly knows. ___
an - oth - er G - Boy will take___ his place. ___
Oo, oo, oo.)
I ain't no glam-

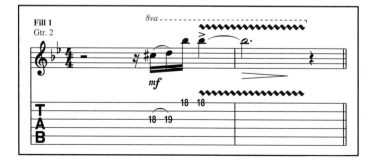

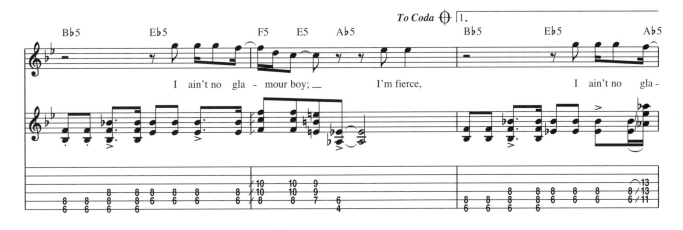

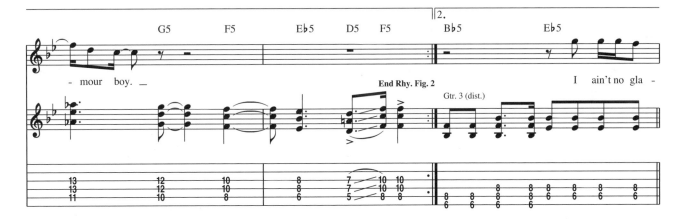

Gtr. 2: w/ Fill 2, 2nd time

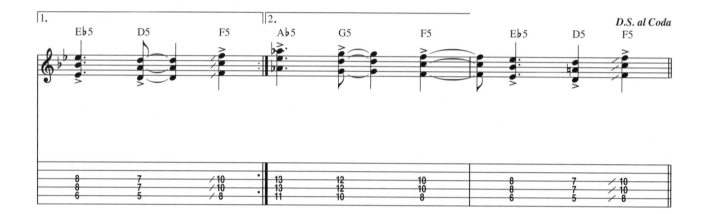

D.S. al Coda

Gtr. 3: w/ Rhy. Fig. 2, last 3 meas., simile

Gtr. 3: w/ Rhy. Fig. 2, simile

Outro-Chorus

I ain't no gla - mour boy. _ Yeah, yeah! _____ I ain't no gla-

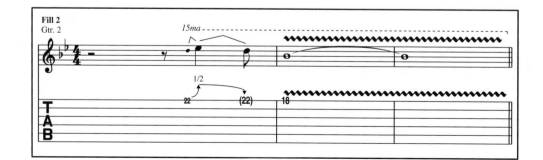

Additional Lyrics

3. The glamour boys don't think about tomorrow,
   The glamour boys just need tonight to play.
   But just like things that can't afford credit,
   Time catches up and you have to pay.
   The glamour boys are always on the guest list,
   You'll always find them in the hottest spots in town.
   They'll be your friend if you have fame of fortune,
   If you don't they won't be hanging 'round.

Gloria

Words and Music by Van Morrison

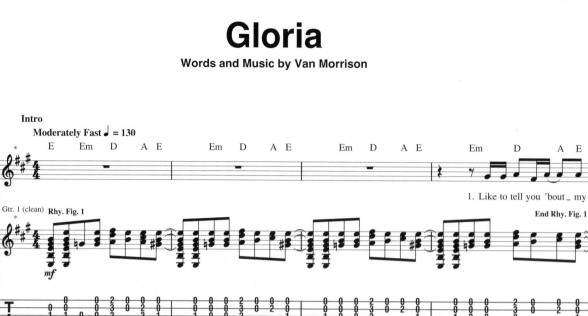

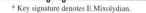

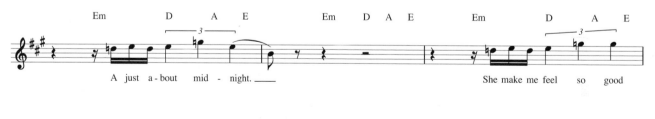

Heartbreaker

Words and Music by Cliff Wade and Geoff Gill

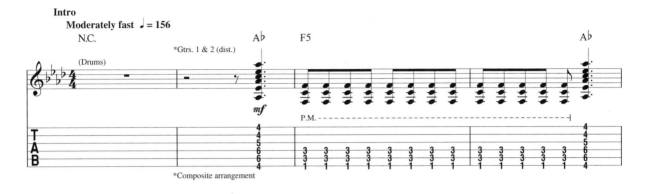

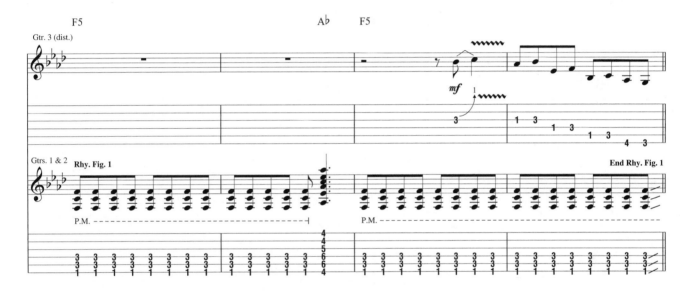

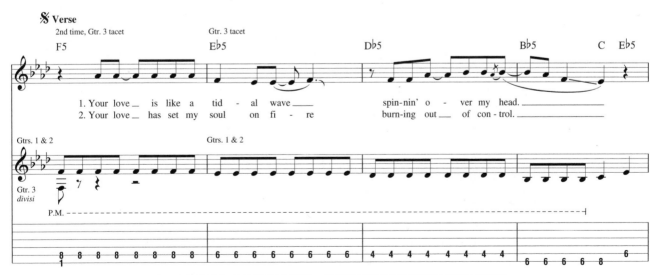

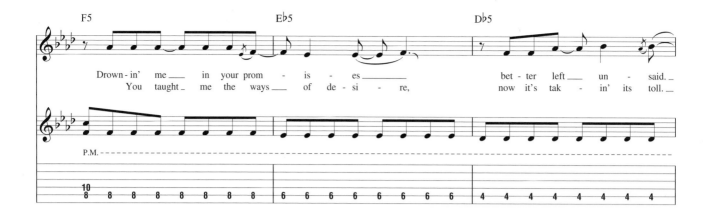

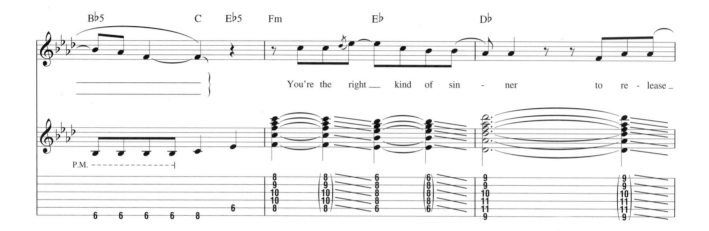

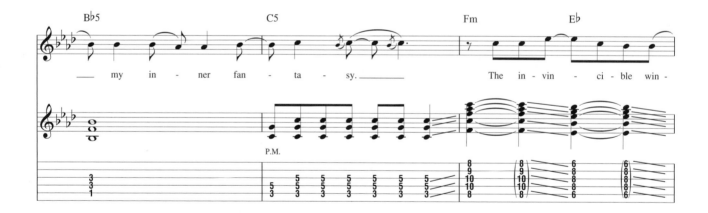

84

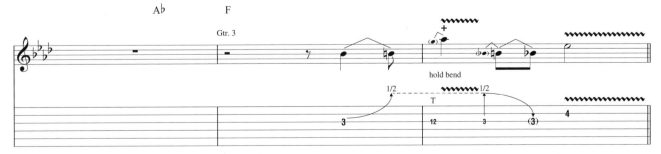

Coda
Chorus
Half-time feel

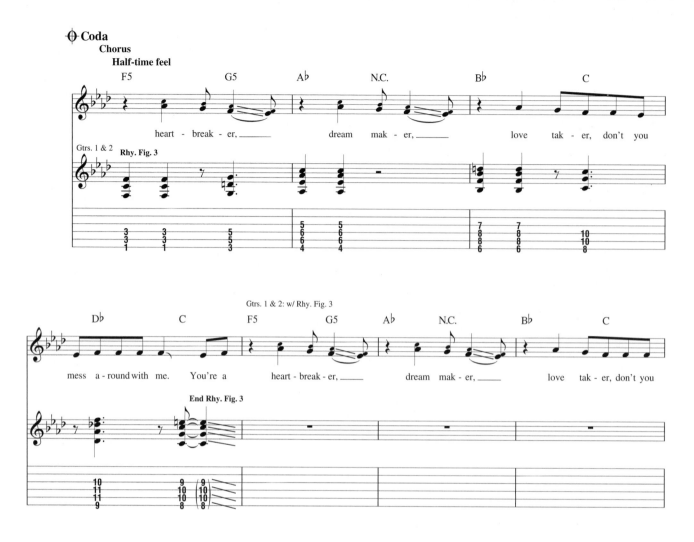

heart - break - er, _____ dream mak - er, _____ love tak - er, don't you

mess a - round with me. You're a heart - break - er, _____ dream mak - er, _____ love tak - er, don't you

Interlude
End half-time feel

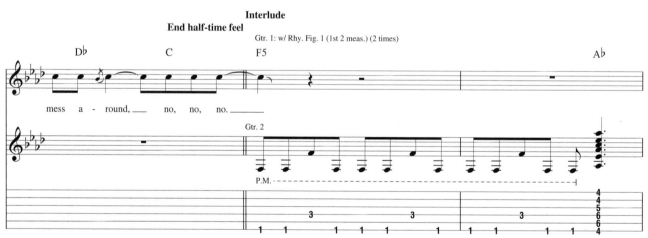

mess a - round, ___ no, no, no. _____

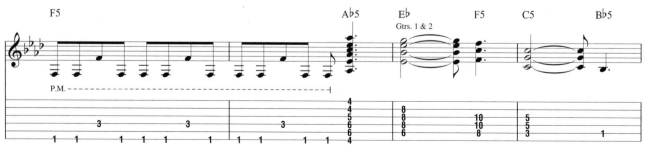

86

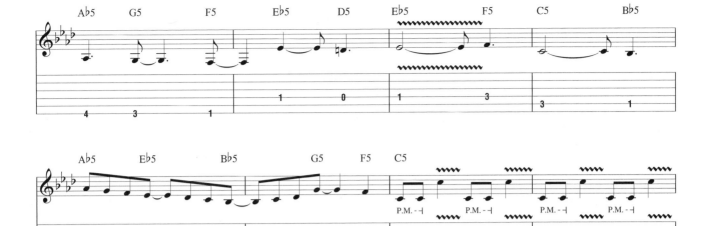

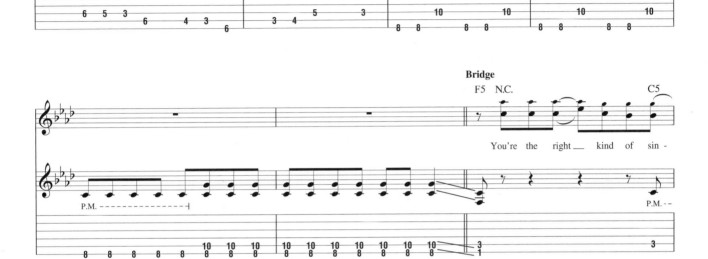

Bridge

You're the right kind of sin-

-ner to re-lease my in-ner fan-ta-sy.

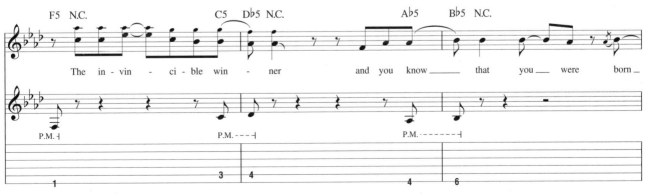

The in-vin-ci-ble win-ner and you know that you were born

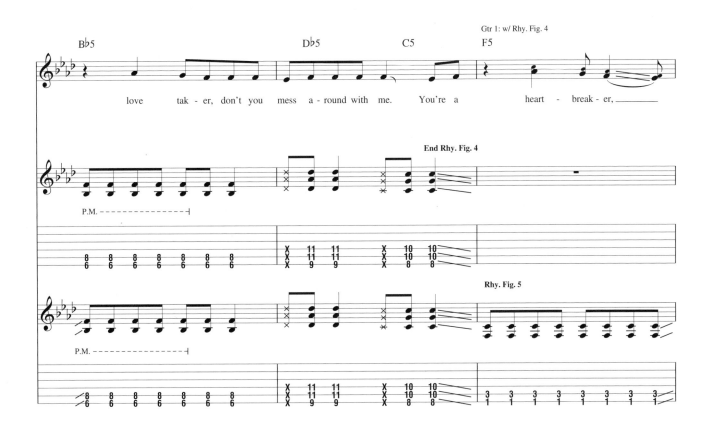

love tak-er, don't you mess a-round with me. You're a heart - break - er, _____

dream mak - er, _____ love tak - er, heart-break - er.

Outro - Guitar Solo

Gtrs. 1 & 2: w/ Rhy Fig. 5

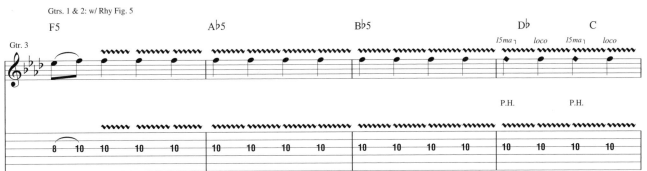

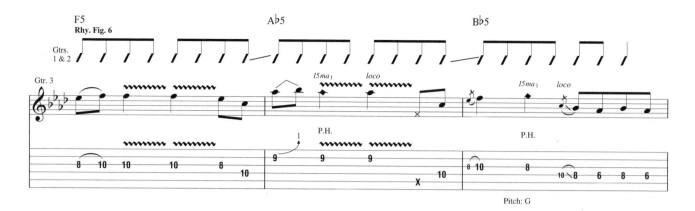

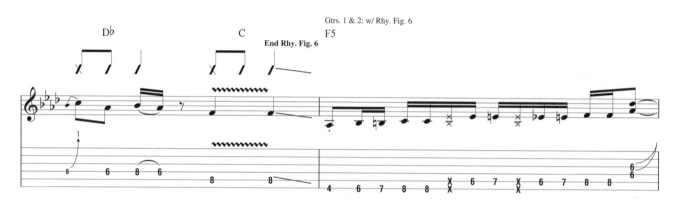

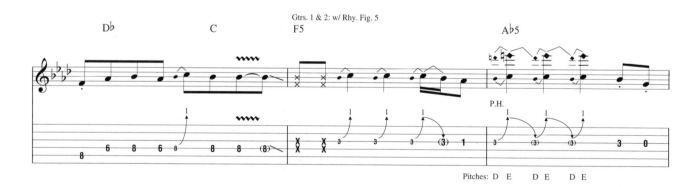

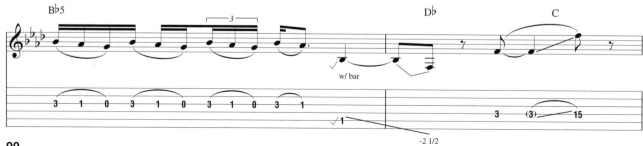

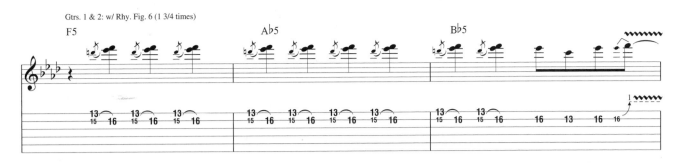

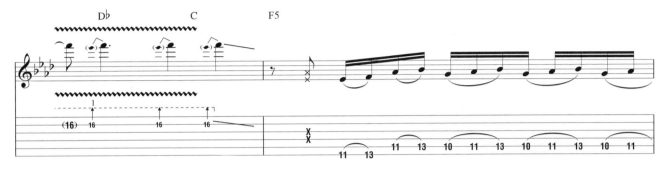

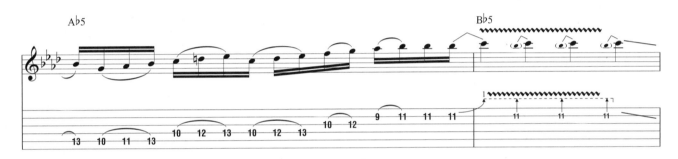

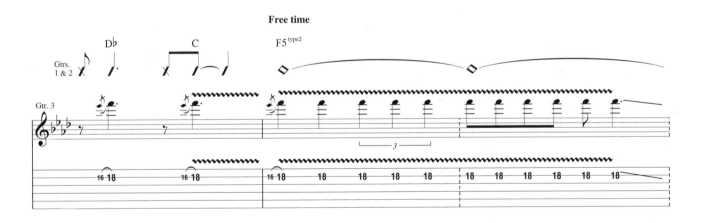

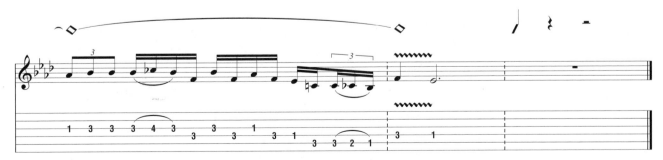

Her Strut

Words and Music by Bob Seger

E5

Tune down 1/2 step:
(low to high) Eb-Ab-Db-Gb-Bb-Eb

Intro
Moderate Rock ♩ = 120

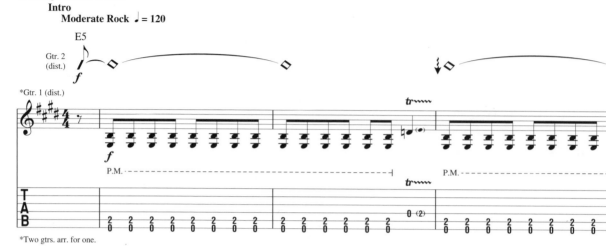

*Two gtrs. arr. for one.

Gtr. 2 tacet

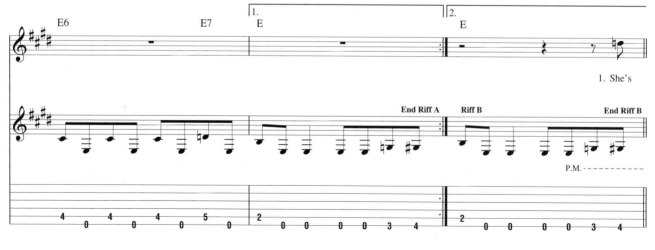

**Chord symbols reflect implied harmony.

1. She's

Chorus

oh, ___   they love ___ to watch her strut.
Oh, ___   they'll love ___ to watch her strut.

Oh, ___   they do ___ re-spect her but ___   they love ___ to watch her
Oh, ___   they'll kill ___ to make the cut, ___   they love ___ to watch her

Interlude

strut. ___   Uh!   Oh, yeah.   Oh. ___
strut. ___   Ah!   Oh, yeah.   Love to watch her.

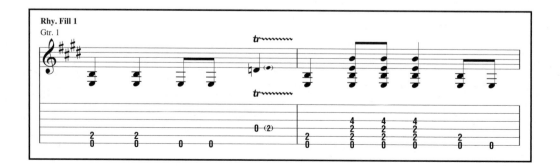

Gtr. 2: w/ Riff D

Gtr. 1: w/ Riff B

2. Some -

Guitar Solo

Gtr. 1: w/ Riff B

Gtr. 1: w/ Riff C

Watch her strut, now.

Gtr. 3 (dist.)

*w/ delay

delay off

*Set for quarter-note regeneration with 2 repeats.

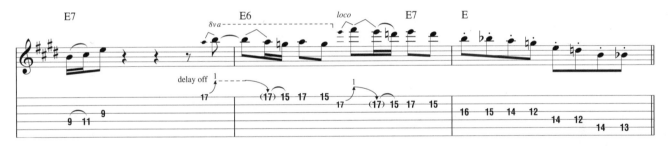

w/ delay

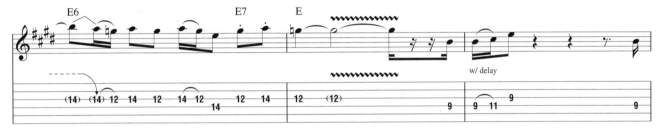

loco

delay off

Chorus

Gtr. 3 tacet

Oh, _____ they love ___ to watch her strut.

Gtr. 3

Gtr. 1

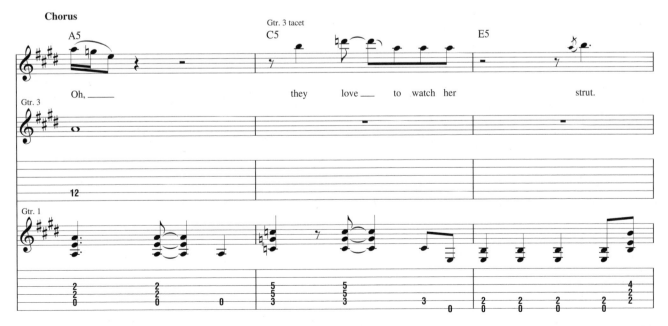

Here I Go Again

Words and Music by Bernie Marsden and David Coverdale

*Chord symbols reflect overall harmony.

*Composite arrangement

Chorus

Gtr. 3 tacet

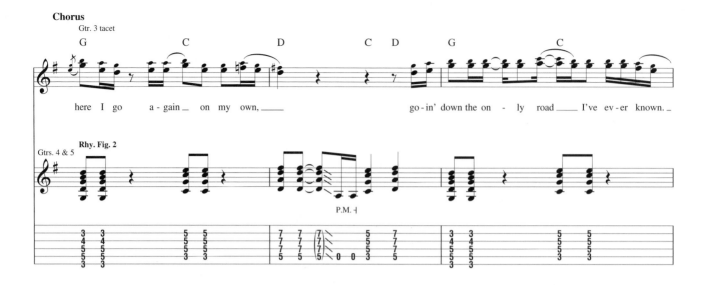

here I go a-gain___ on my own,___ go-in' down the on - ly road___ I've ev-er known.___

Rhy. Fig. 2

Gtrs. 4 & 5

P.M.

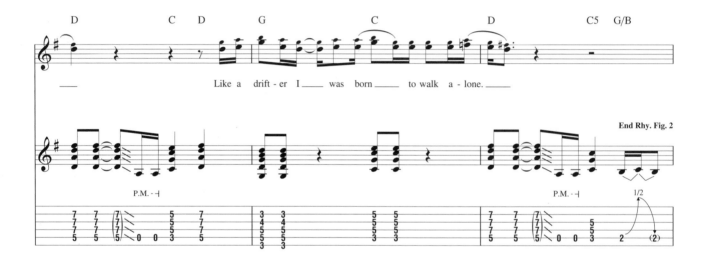

Like a drift-er I ___ was born ___ to walk a - lone. ___

P.M.

End Rhy. Fig. 2

P.M.

1/2

And I've made up my mind,___ I ain't wast - in' no more time.___

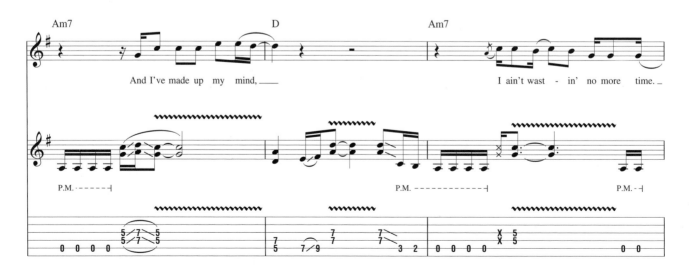

P.M.

P.M.

P.M.

Pre-Chorus

rest of my days. ___ 'Cause I know what it means ___ to

walk a - long ___ the lone - ly street ___ of dreams. ___ And

Chorus

here I go a - gain ___ on my own, ___ go - in' down the on - ly road ___ I've ev - er known. ___

___ Like a drift - er I ___ was born ___ to walk a - lone. ___

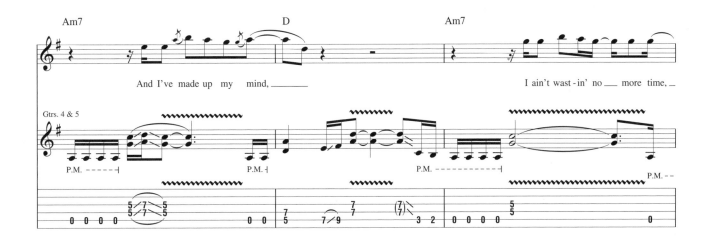

And I've made up my mind, _____

I ain't wast-in' no ___ more time, _

Gtrs. 4 & 5

P.M. ------| P.M. -| P.M. ------------| P.M. --

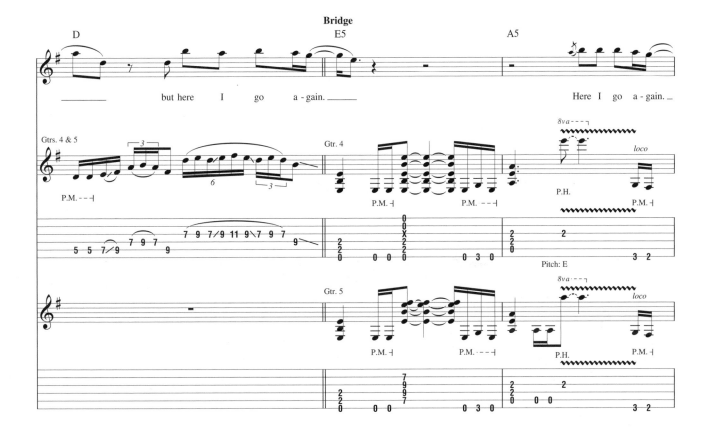

Bridge

_____ but here I go a-gain. ____

Here I go a-gain. _

Gtrs. 4 & 5

P.M. --| P.M. -| P.M. ---| P.H. P.M. -|

Gtr. 4

Pitch: E

Gtr. 5

P.M. -| P.M. ---| P.H. P.M. -|

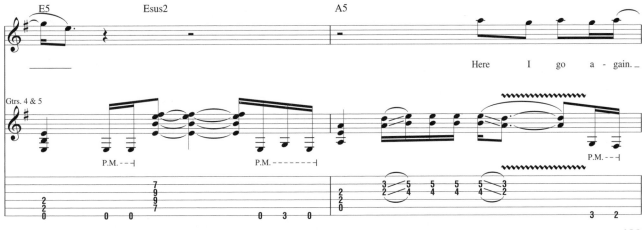

_____ Here I go a-gain. _

Gtrs. 4 & 5

P.M. --- | P.M. ---------| P.M. ---|

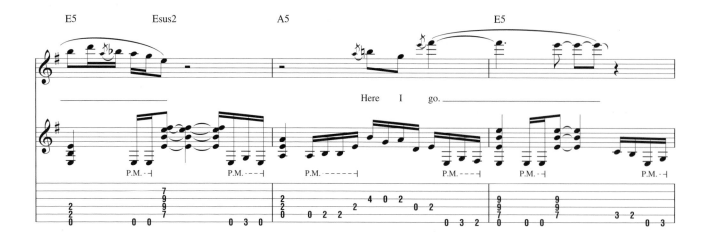

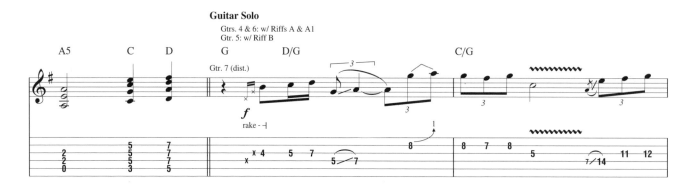

Here I go.

Guitar Solo

Gtrs. 4 & 6: w/ Riffs A & A1
Gtr. 5: w/ Riff B

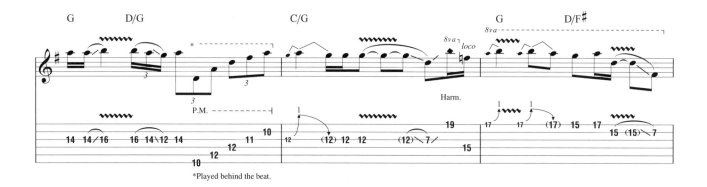

*Played behind the beat.

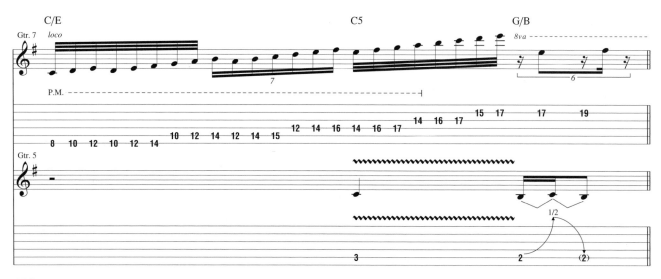

Hey Lawdy Mama

Words and Music by Jerry Edmonton, John Kay and Larry Byrom

1. You'd like to show me all a-round. Thank you girl but I know this town
2. This town is bor - ing you to tears, noth-ing in the world ev - er hap - ens here.

* Use notes in parenthesis on repeats of Rhy. Fig. only.

Hey Nineteen

Words and Music by Walter Becker and Donald Fagen

Verse

Gtr. 4 tacet

Rhy. Fig. 2

1. Way _ back _ when _ in six - ty sev - en,

I _ was _ the dan - dy of Gam - ma Chi. _

Sweet things _ from Bos - ton, so young and will - ing,

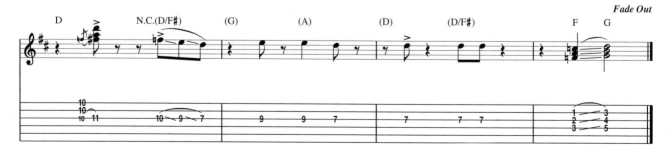

118

Hungry

Words and Music by Mike Tramp and Vito Bratta

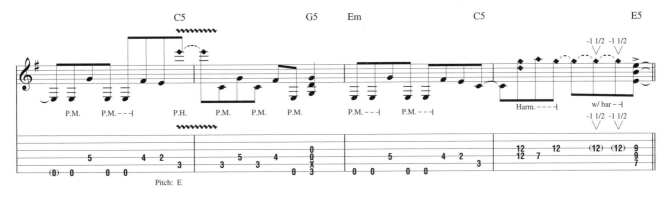

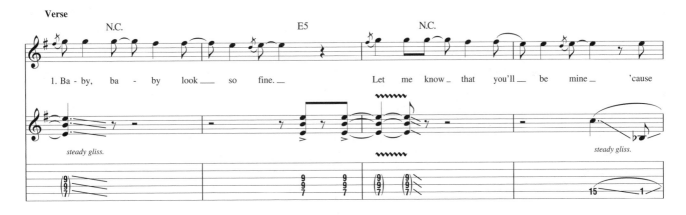

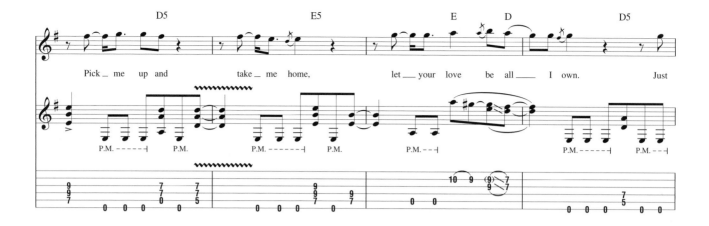

Pick me up and take me home, let your love be all I own. Just

be my ba - by through the night. Ba - by,

Pre-Chorus

2nd time, Gtr. 1: w/ Fill 1

take off all your leath - er, and show me all your lace.

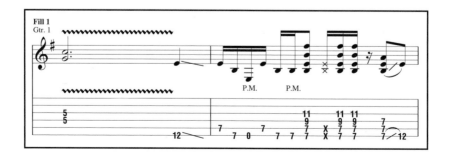

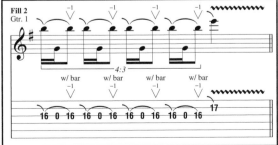

Guitar Solo

Gtr. 5 tacet

3. Keep your en- gine run- nin' high _____ when you take ___ my love ___ in- side. ___

I Wanna Rock

Words and Music by D. Snider

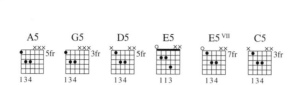

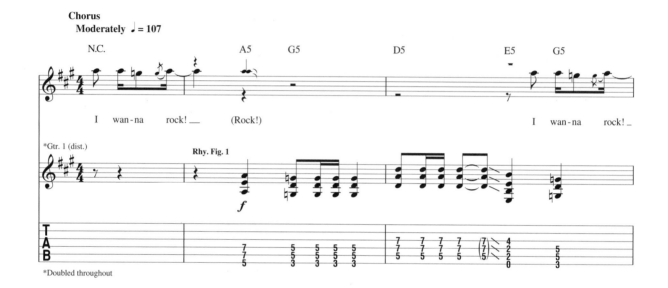

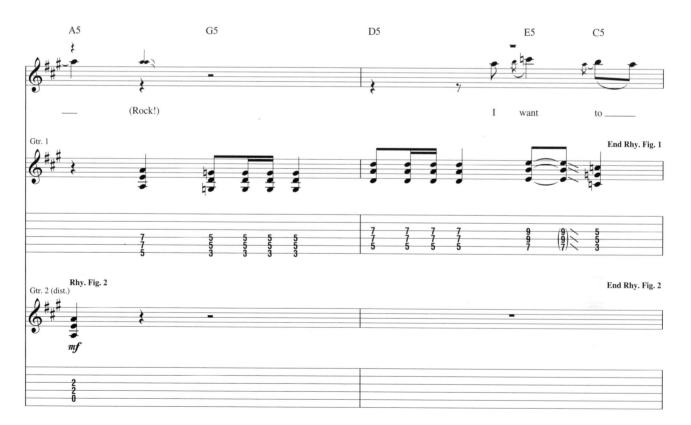

129

Guitar Solo

*See top of first page of song for chord diagrams pertaining to rhythm slashes.

I wan-na rock!

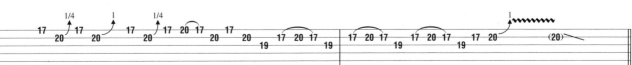

131

I'm Bad, I'm Nationwide

Words and Music by Billy F Gibbons, Dusty Hill and Frank Lee Beard

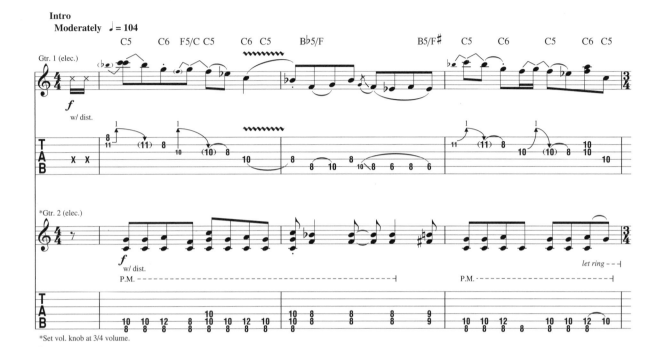

*Set vol. knob at 3/4 volume.

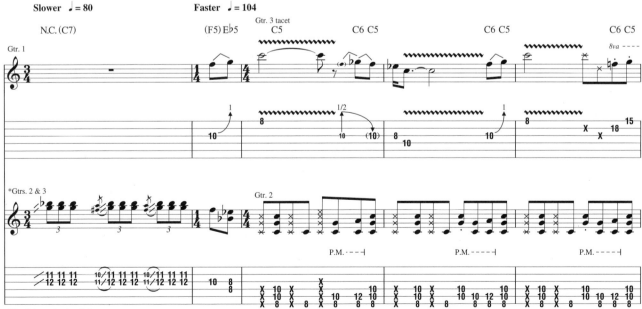

*Gtr. 3 (acous.) - played **f**.

134

new Ca - dil - lac,_____ I had a fine fox in front, I had three more in the back. They

sport - in' short dress - es, wear - in' spike - heel shoes,_____ they smok - in' Luck - y Strikes and wear - in'

Chorus

Gtr. 1: w/ Rhy. Fig. 1

ny - lons _____ too. 'Cause we bad, _____ we na - tion - wide. _____

*As before

Yeah, we bad, _____

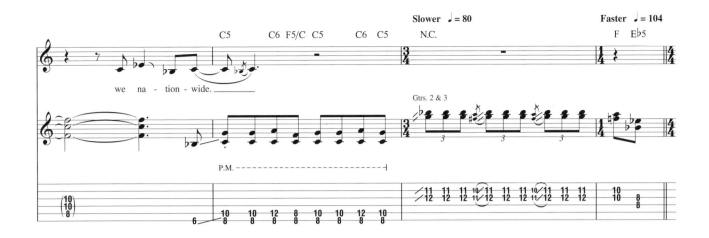

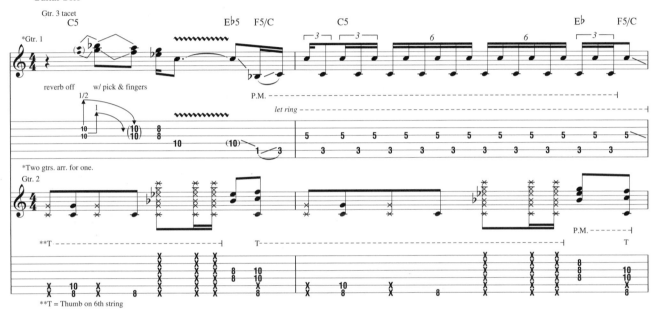

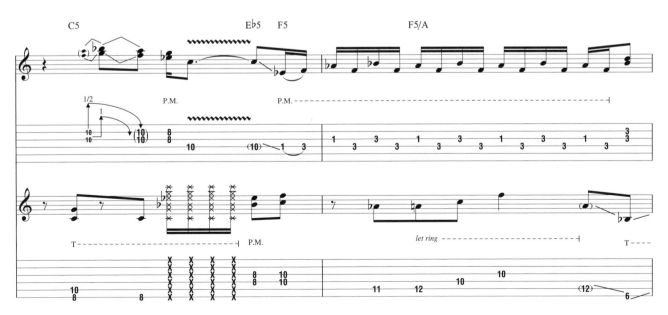

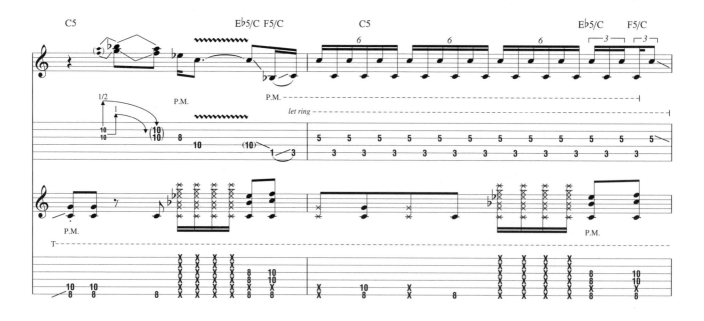

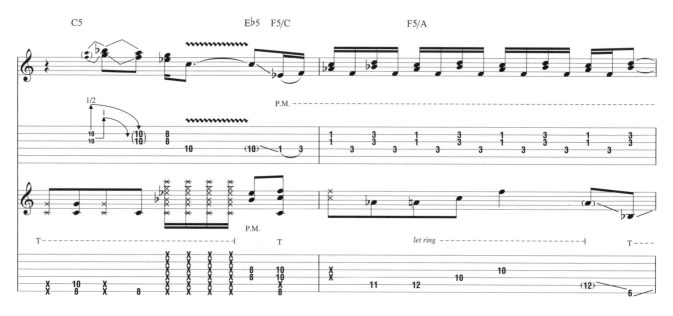

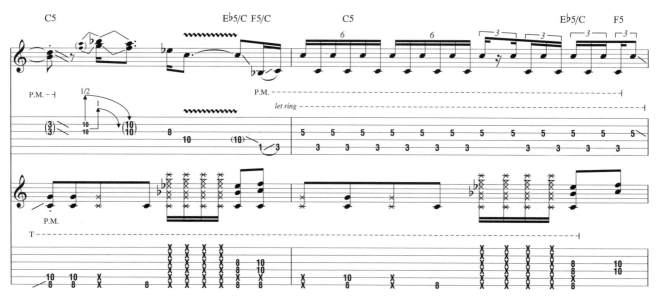

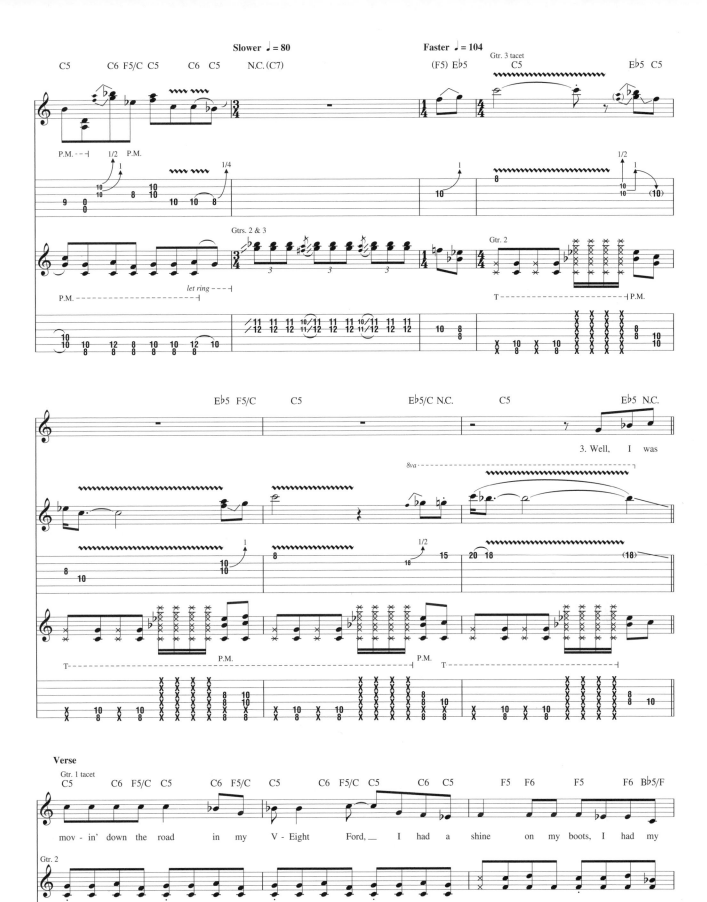

142

Outro-Guitar Solo

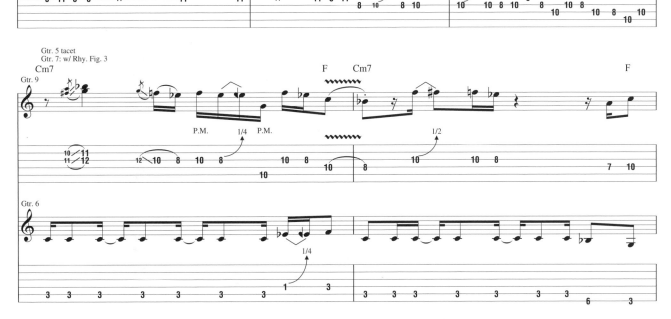

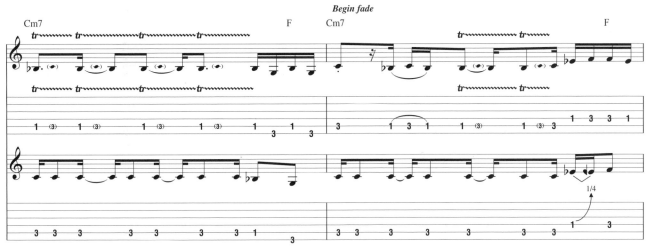

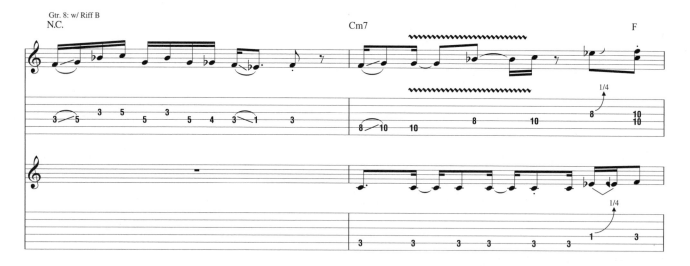

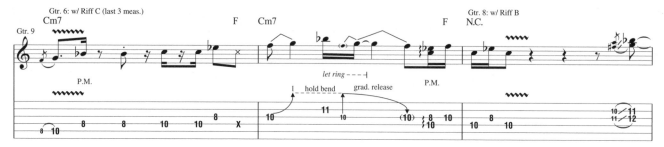

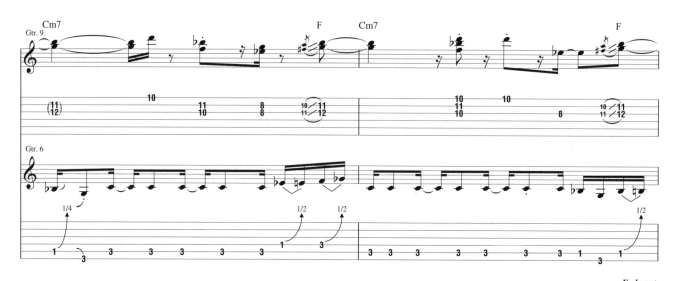

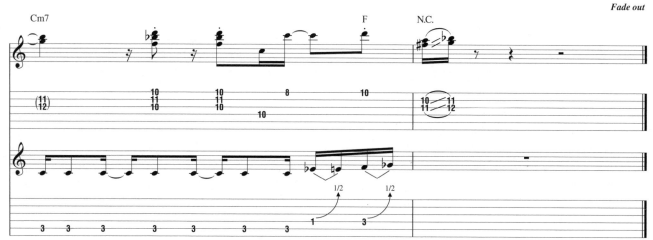

I'm Eighteen

Words and Music by Alice Cooper, Michael Bruce, Glen Buxton, Dennis Dunaway and Neal Smith

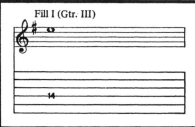

(resume Rhy. Fig. 4)

Took eight-een years to get this far.   Don't al-ways know what I'm

talk-in' a-bout.   Feels like I'm liv-in' in the mid-dle of doubt. 'Cause I'm

Chorus
w/*Rhy. Figs. 1 & 1A (both 3 times)

eight-een.   I get con-fused ev-'ry day.   Eight-een. I just don't

*w/slight variations ad lib. (both gtrs.)

know what to say.   Eight-een. I got-ta get a-way.

w/*Rhy. Fig. 2 (Gtr. II)

Gtr. I

Gtr. III

*w/slight variations ad lib.

3rd Verse
w/*Rhy. Fig. 4

Woh.   Lines form on my face and my hands.

*Refers to Gtr. IV only.

150

Lines form— on the left and right.— I'm in the mid - dle, the

mid - dle of life.— I'm a boy and I'm a man. I'm eight - een and I

Chorus
w/*Rhy. Figs. 1 (2 times) & 1A (3 times)

like it! Yes, I like—

*w/slight variations ad lib. (both gtrs.)

It Can Happen

Words and Music by John Anderson, Trevor Rabin and Chris Squire

*Elec. sitar arr. for gtr.

**Chord symbols reflect implied harmony.

***Synth. arr. for gtr.

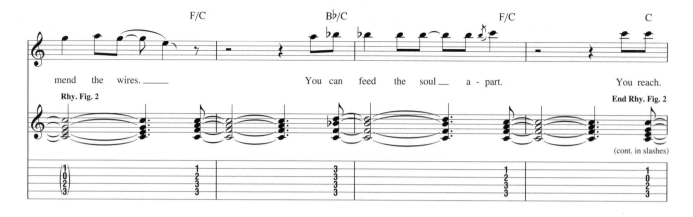

mend the wires. _____ You can feed the soul _____ a - part. You reach.

Rhy. Fig. 2

End Rhy. Fig. 2

(cont. in slashes)

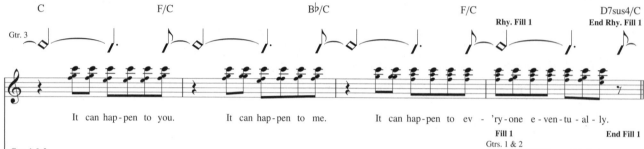

Gtr. 3

It can hap-pen to you. It can hap-pen to me. It can hap-pen to ev - 'ry-one e - ven-tu - al - ly.

Fill 1

End Fill 1

Gtrs. 1 & 2

Gtr. 4 (elec.)
divisi

Fill 1A

End Fill 1A

mf
w/ clean tone
& chorus

Interlude

Gtrs. 1 & 2 tacet

Gtr. 4

P.M. - - - - - - - - - - - - - - - - -

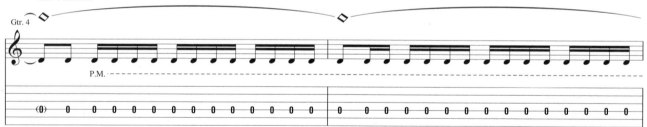

(It's a co...

It's a

P.M. -

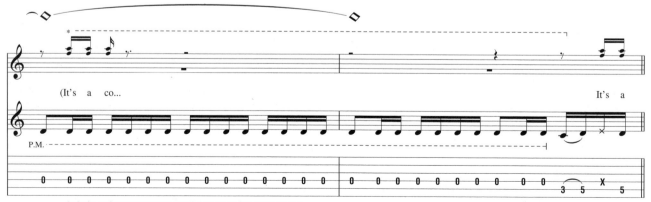

*w/ echo set for quarter-note regeneration; gradually fade in echo repeats.

Verse

D7sus4/C

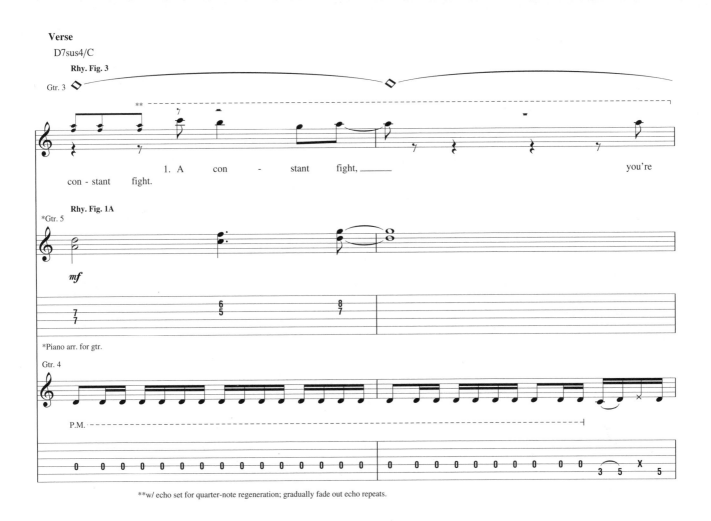

con - stant fight.

**w/ echo set for quarter-note regeneration; gradually fade out echo repeats.

***Fade in echo as before.

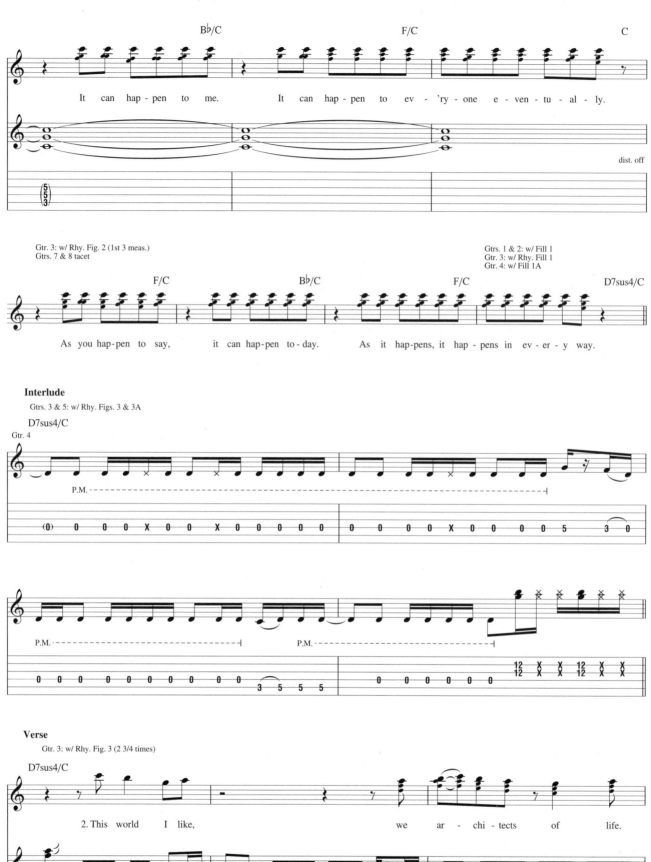

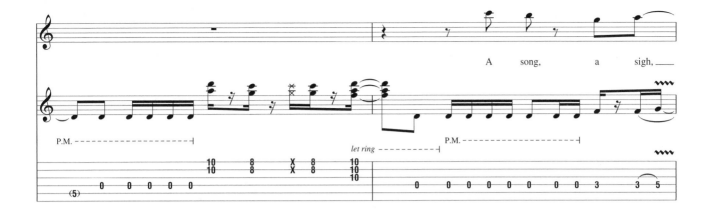

A song, a sigh,

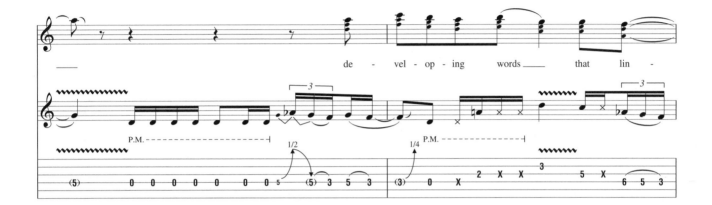

de - vel - op - ing words ____ that lin -

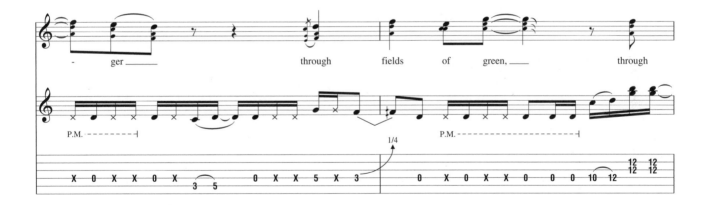

- ger ____ through fields of green, ____ through

o - pen eyes; ____ this for us ____ to see. ____

Pre-Chorus

*Gtr. 4 to left of slash in tab.

Gtr. 6 tacet

There's a cra‑zy world out‑side, we're not a‑bout to lose our pride.

let ring

w/ dist.

Gtrs. 1 & 2

P.S.

Chorus

Gtrs. 1 & 2: w/ Riff A (2 1/2 times)
Gtr. 3: w/ Rhy. Fig. 1

Voc. Fig. 1

End Voc. Fig. 1

It can hap‑pen to you. It can hap‑pen to me. It can hap‑pen to ev‑'ry‑one e‑ven‑tu‑al‑ly.

Gtrs. 7 & 8

Gtr. 3: w/ Rhy. Fig. 2 (1 1/2 times)
Gtrs. 7 & 8 tacet

Voc. Fig. 2

As you hap‑pen to say, it can hap‑pen to‑day. As it hap‑pens, it hap‑

End Voc. Fig. 2   Voc. Fig. 3

pens in ev‑er‑y way. As you hap‑pen to see, it will hap‑pen to be.

Gtr. 8

Gtr. 7
divisi

P.S.

161

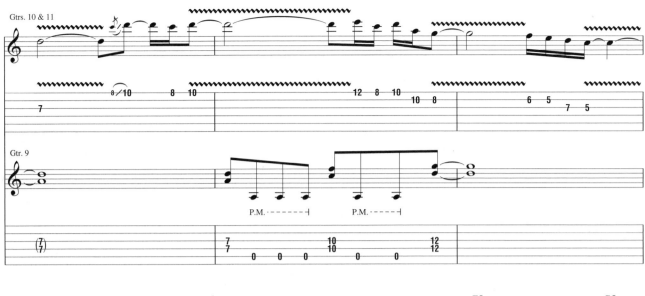

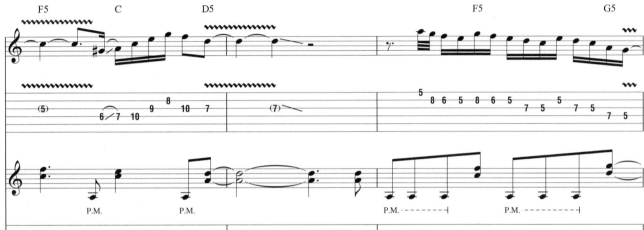

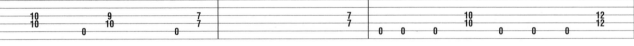

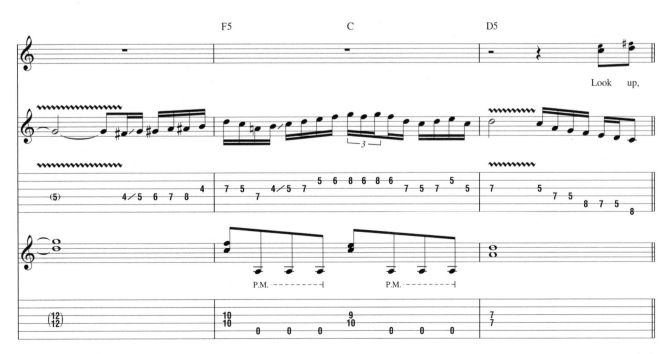

Pre-Chorus

look down._____ There's a cra - zy world _ out - side, we're not a - bout _ to lose _ our pride.

Interlude

It can

Chorus

hap - pen to you, it can hap - pen to me. It can hap - pen to you, it can

(It can hap - pen to you, it can hap - pen to me, it can hap - pen to ev -

hap - pen to me. It can hap - pen to you, it can hap - pen to me. It can

'ry - one e - ven - tu - al - ly. As you hap - pen to see, it will hap - pen to be,

hap - pen to you.   ...no - where and no - where.

noth - ing hap - pens to no - where and no - where.

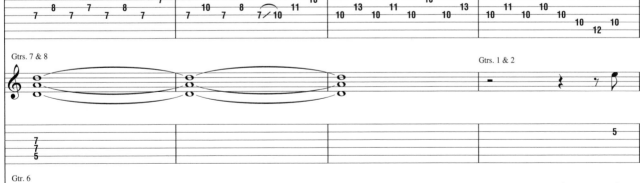

Interlude

You can

165

Outro-Chorus

Bkgd. Voc.: w/ Voc. Fig. 1
Gtrs. 1 & 2: w/ Riff A (till fade)
Gtr. 3: w/ Rhy. Fig. 1
Gtr. 12 tacet

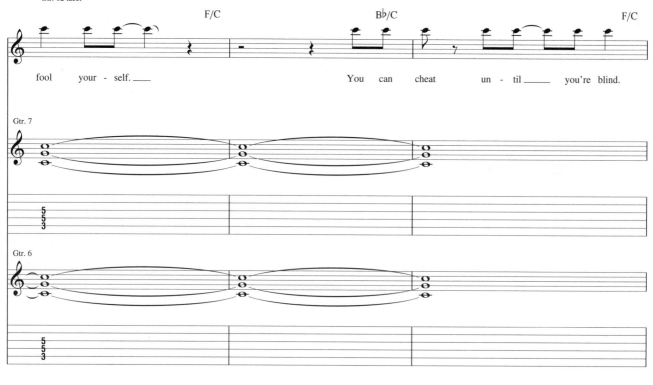

fool your - self. ___ You can cheat un - til ___ you're blind.

Gtrs. 6 & 7 tacet

Bkgd. Voc.: w/ Voc. Fig. 2
Gtr. 3: w/ Rhy. Fig. 2 (till fade)

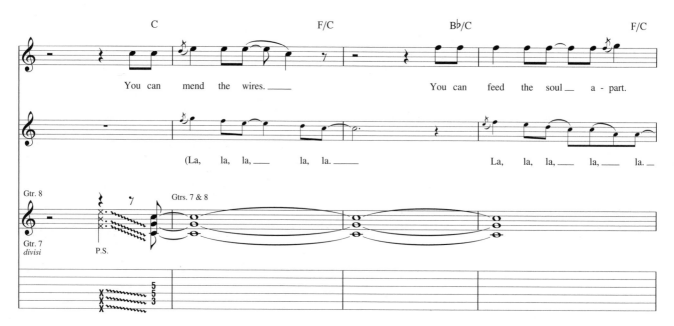

You can cut your heart, it can hap - pen.

You can mend the wires. ___ You can feed the soul ___ a - part.

(La, la, la, ___ la, la. ___ La, la, la, ___ la, ___ la.

It's So Easy

Words and Music by W. Axl Rose, Slash, Izzy Stradlin', Duff McKagan, Steven Adler and West Arkeen

Verse

1. I see your sis-ter in her Sun-day dress. __ She's out to please, she pouts __

2. Cars are crash-in' ev-'ry night. I drink 'n' drive, ev-'ry-thing's __ in sight. __ I

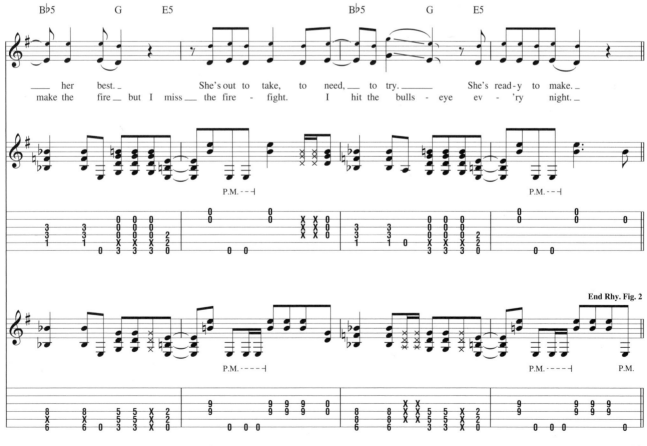

__ her best. __ She's out to take, to need, to try. _____ She's read-y to make. __

make the fire __ but I miss __ the fire - fight. I hit the bulls - eye ev - 'ry night. __

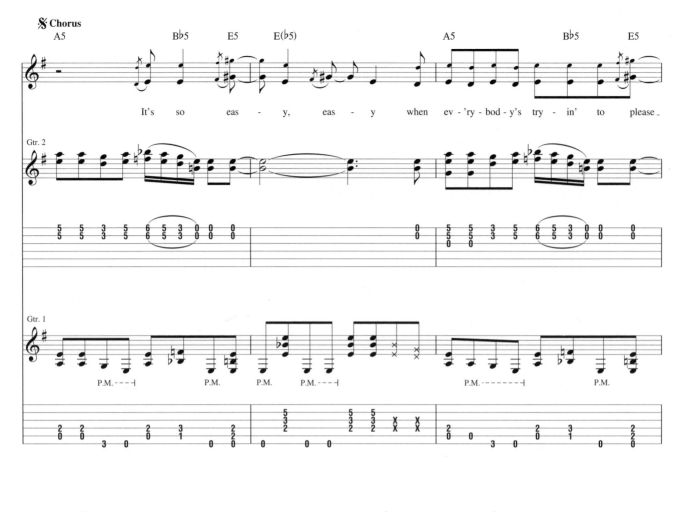

It's so eas - y, eas - y when ev - 'ry-bod-y's try-in' to please ___

___ me, ba - by.

1., 3. It's so eas - y,} eas - y when
2. Yeah, it's so eas - y,}

Bridge

Guitar Solo

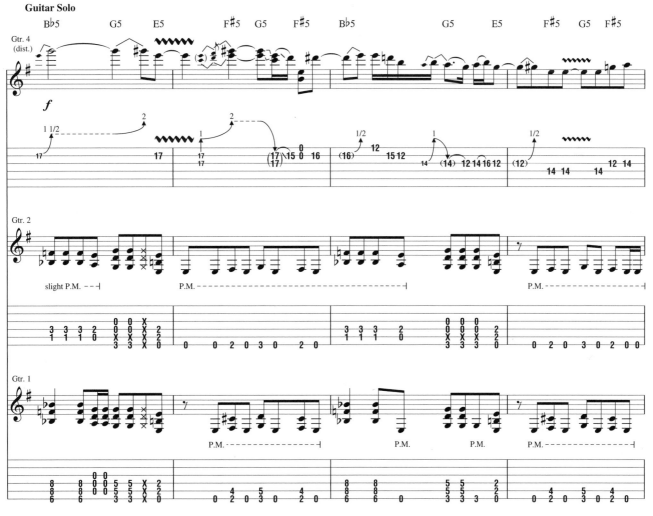

Verse

3. Ya get

noth - in' for noth - in' if that's ___ what ya do. ___ Turn a - round ___ bitch, I got a ___ use for ___ you. ___ Be - sides,

174

you ain't got noth-in' bet-ter to do and I'm bored.

Coda

Gtr. 2: w/ Riff A (2 times)

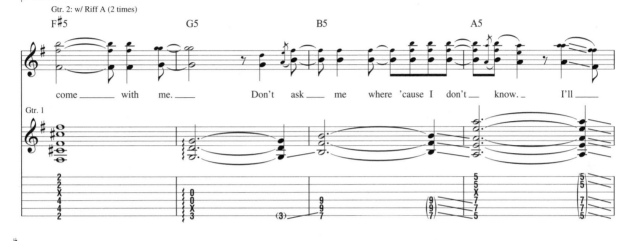

come with me. Don't ask me where 'cause I don't know. I'll

try to please you. I ain't got no mon-ey but it goes to show...

Outro-Guitar Solo

Gtr. 1: w/ Rhy. Fig. 2 (1st 4 meas., 4 times)
Gtr. 2: w/ Rhy. Fig. 1 (4 times)

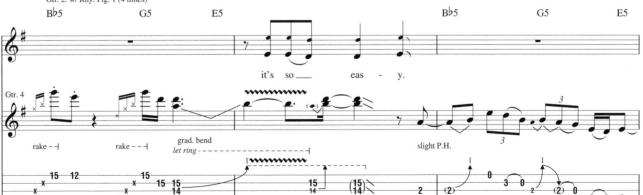

it's so eas-y.

175

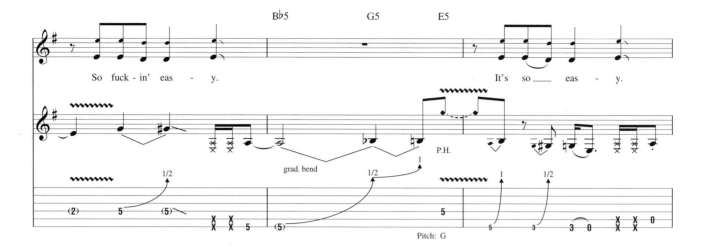

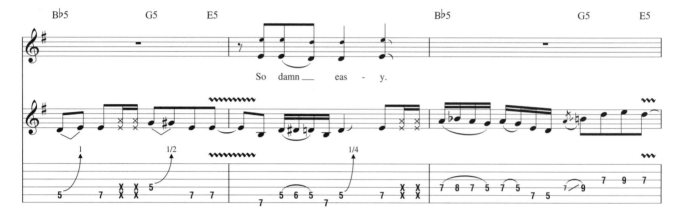

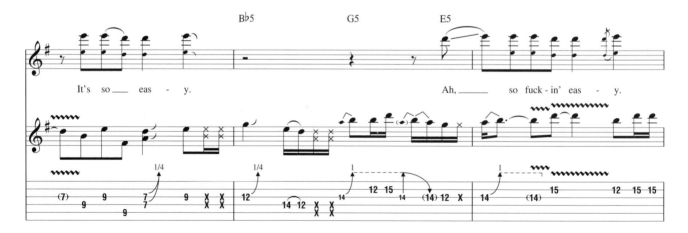

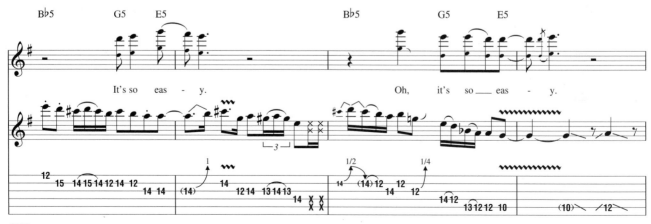

Jet Airliner

Words and Music by Paul Pena

*Composite arrangement

**Symbols in parentheses represent chord names respective to capoed guitar.
Chord symbols reflect basic harmony.

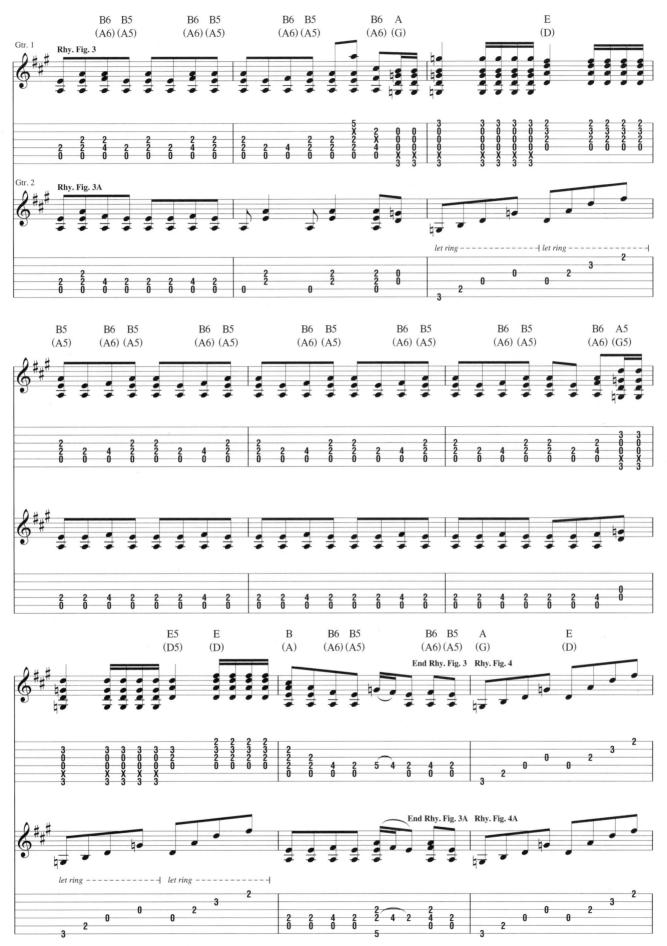

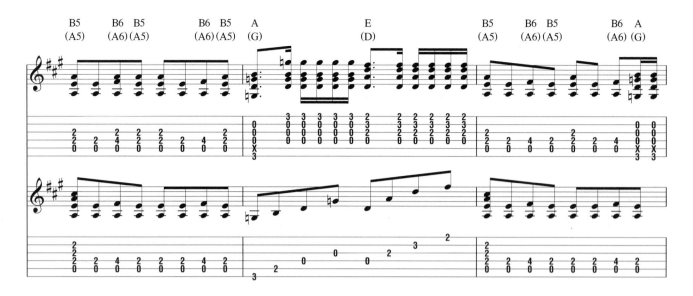

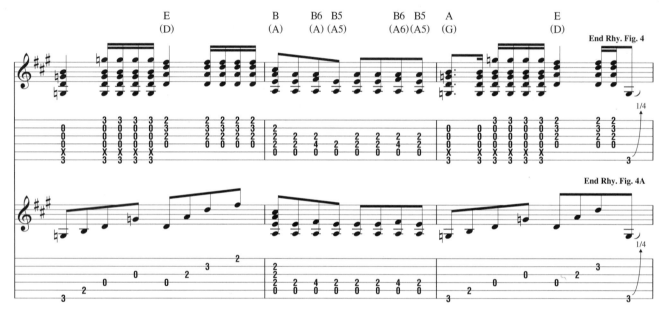

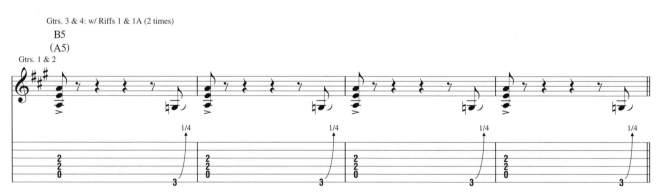

Gtrs. 3 & 4: w/ Riffs 1 & 1A (2 times)

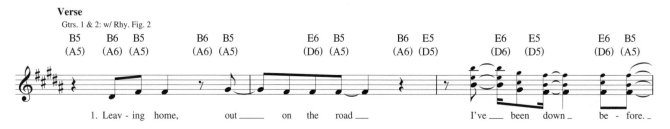

Verse

Gtrs. 1 & 2: w/ Rhy. Fig. 2

B5	B6	B5		B6	B5		E6	B5		B6	E5		E6		E5		E6	B5
(A5)	(A6)	(A5)		(A6)	(A5)		(D6)	(A5)		(A6)	(D5)		(D6)		(D5)		(D6)	(A5)

1. Leav - ing home, out ___ on the road ___   I've ___ been down _ be - fore. _

182

Chorus
Gtr. 2: w/ Rhy. Fig. 4

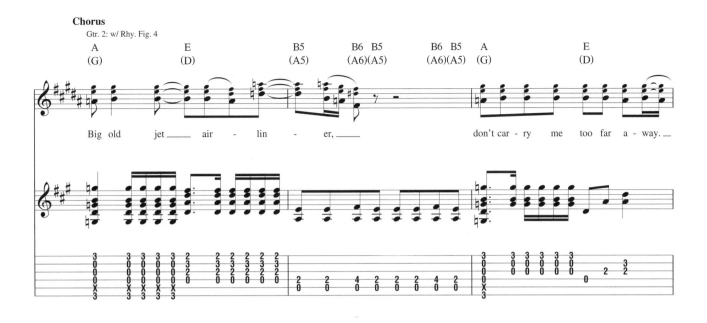

Big old jet___ air-lin-er,___ don't car-ry me too far a-way.___

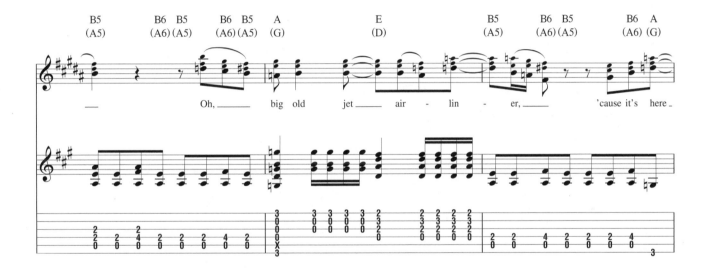

Oh,___ big old jet___ air-lin-er,___ 'cause it's here_

1.

Gtrs. 3 & 4: w/ Riffs A & A1

2.

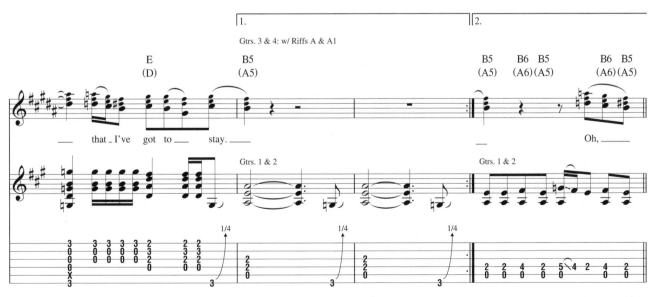

___ that _ I've got to ___ stay.___

Oh,___

Gtrs. 1 & 2

Gtrs. 1 & 2

1/4 1/4 1/4

183

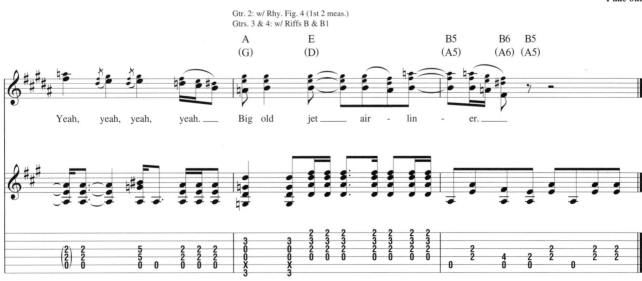

Little Miss Strange

Words and Music by Noel Redding

Verse

3. Lit-tle Miss Strange ___ came out of the dark - ness, walked a-cross my head, I stood be-neath the lights. I'm

* w/ tone control rolled
back to bass position.

Guitar Solo

Locomotive Breath

Words and Music by Ian Anderson

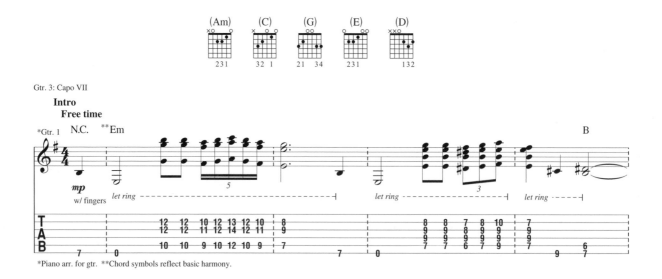

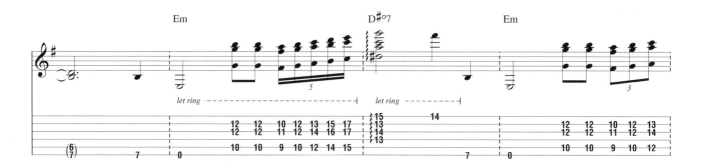

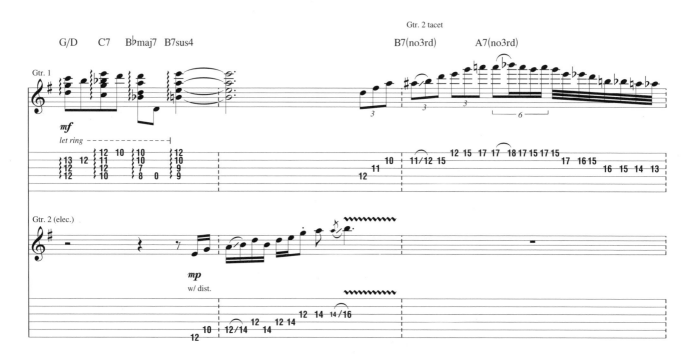

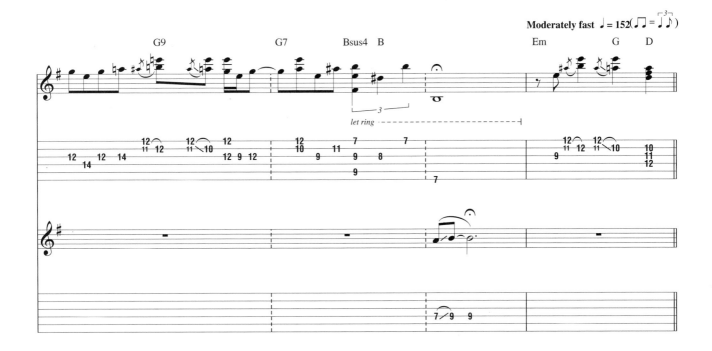

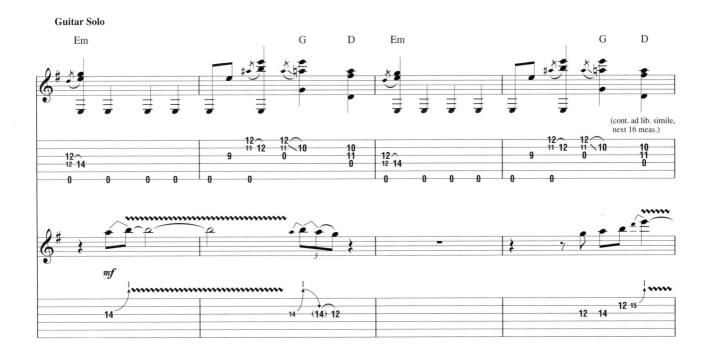

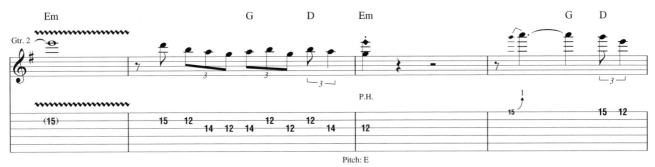

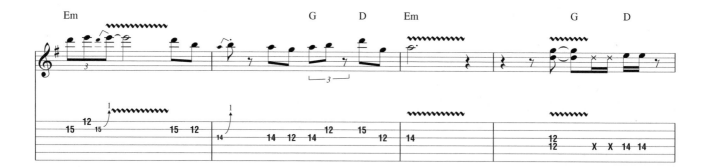

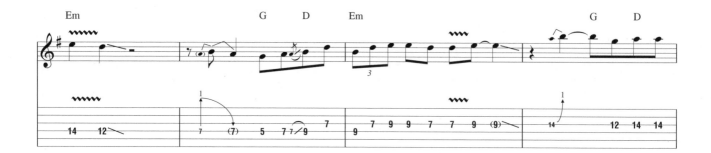

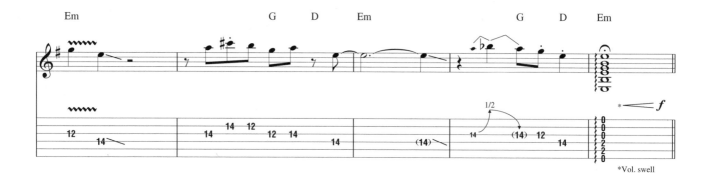

*Vol. swell

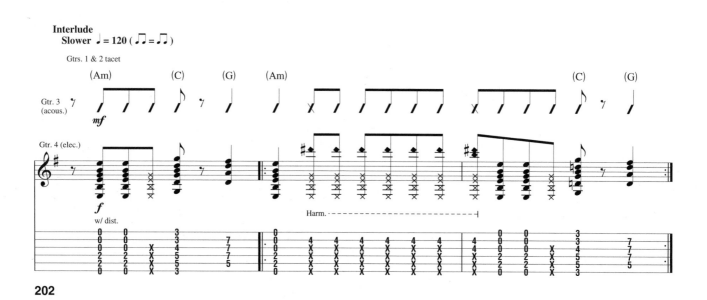

head - long to _____ his death. Oh, _____ he feels the pis - ton scrap-

-ing, steam _____ break - ing on _____ his brow. _____ Old

204

Char - lie stole _ the _ han - dle, and the train, _ it won't _ stop

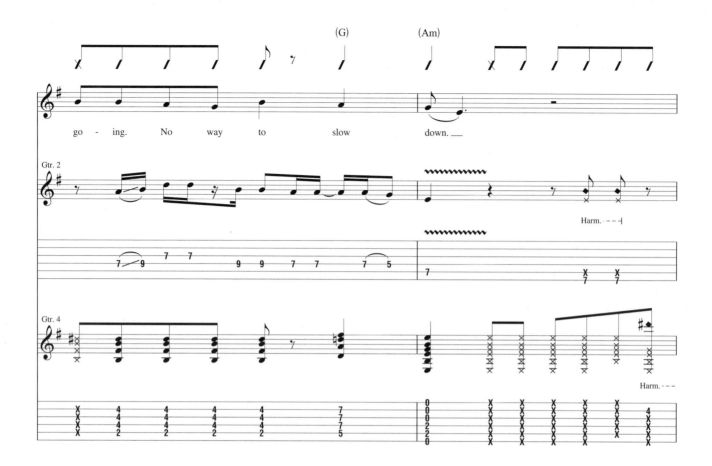

go - ing. No way to slow down. ___

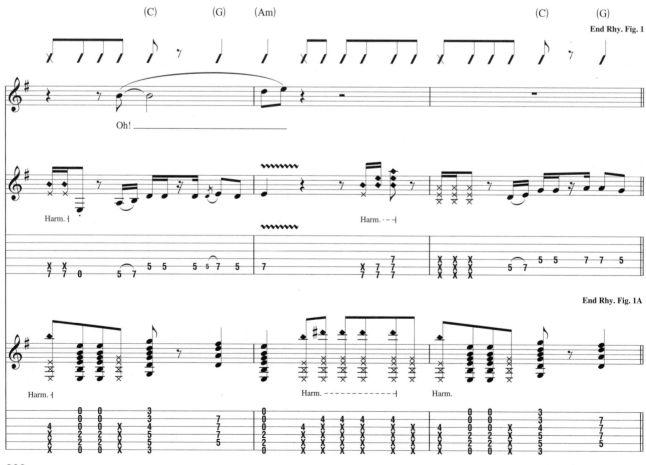

Oh! ___

Gtrs. 3 & 4: w/ Rhy. Figs. 1 & 1A

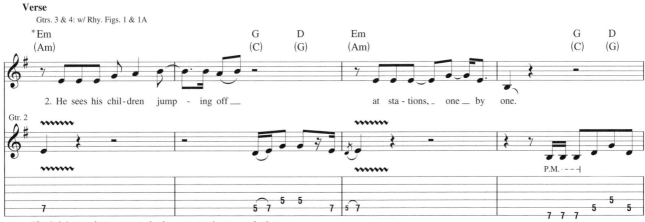

2. He sees his chil-dren jump-ing off ___ at sta-tions, _ one _ by one.

*Symbols in parentheses represent chord names respective to capoed guitar.
Symbols above reflect actual sounding chords.

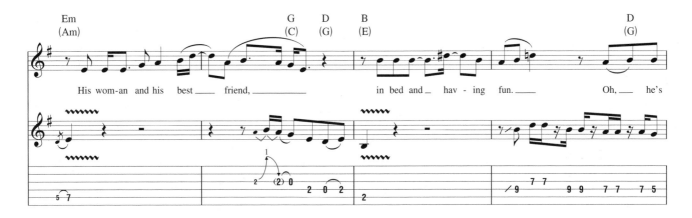

His wom-an and his best ___ friend, _____ in bed and _ hav-ing fun. ___ Oh, ___ he's

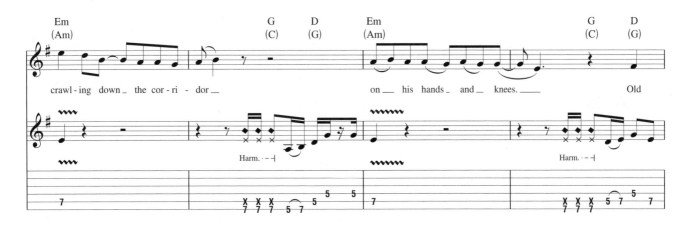

crawl-ing down _ the cor-ri - dor ___ on _ his hands _ and _ knees. ___ Old

Gtrs. 5 & 6: w/ Fills 1 & 1A

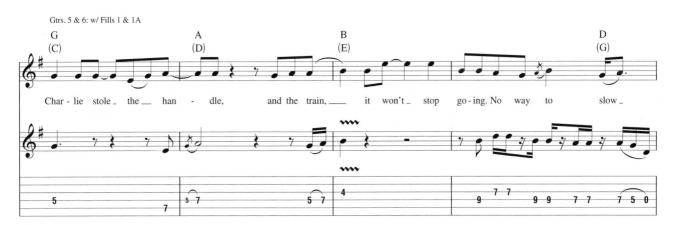

Char - lie stole _ the _ han - dle, ___ and the train, ___ it won't _ stop go-ing. No way to _ slow _

Flute Solo

Gtrs. 3 & 4: w/ Rhy. Figs. 1 & 1A

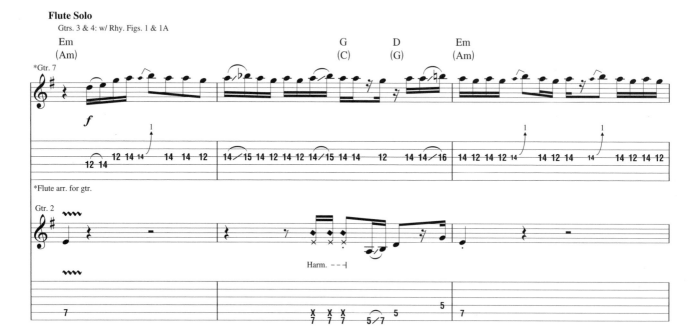

*Flute arr. for gtr.

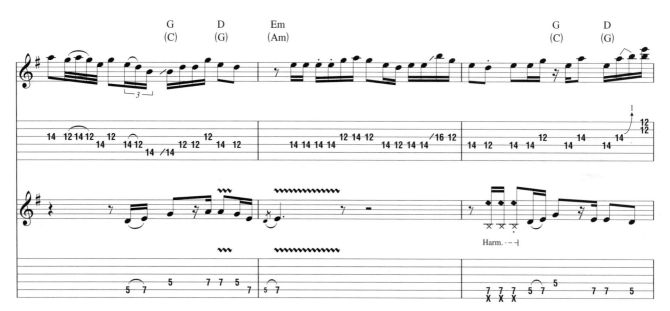

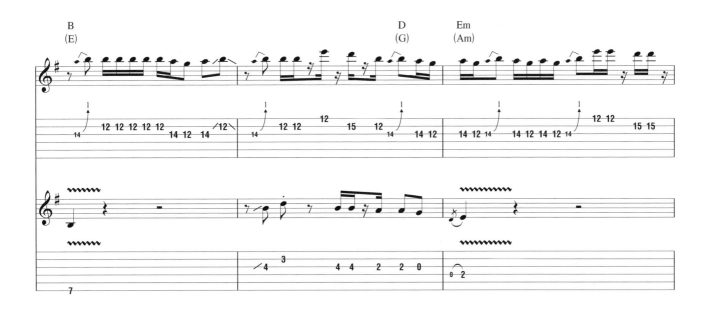

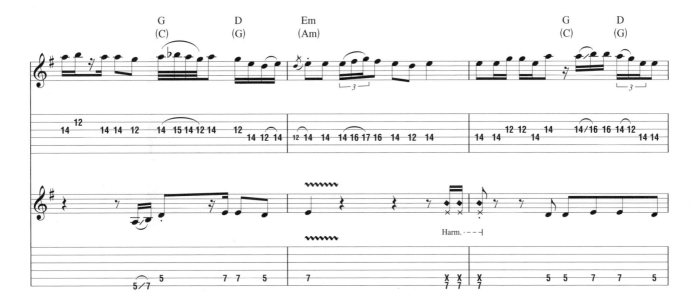

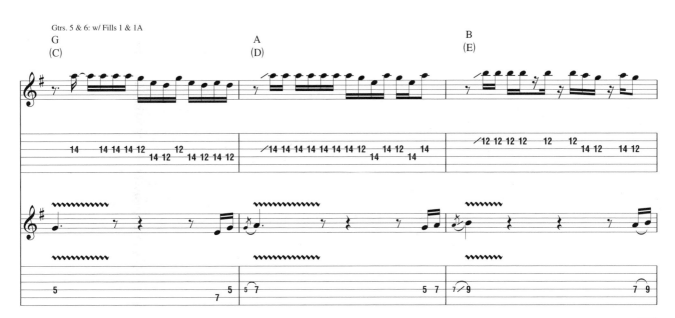

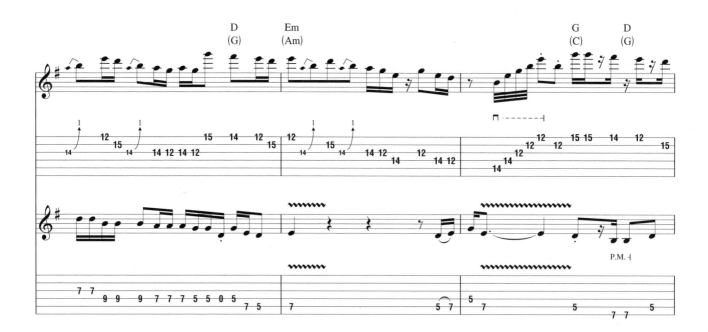

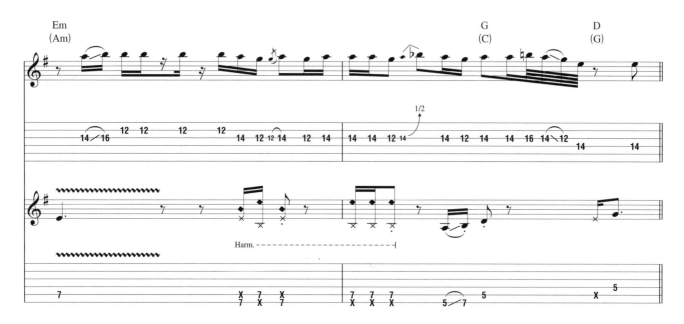

Verse

Gtrs. 3 & 4: w/ Rhy. Figs. 1 & 1A (1st 12 meas.)
Gtr. 7 tacet

3. He hears the si-lence howl-ing, __ catch-es an-gels __ as they fall. __

And the all-time win - ner ___ has got him ___ by ___ the balls. ___ Oh, ___ he

picks up Gid - 'on's Bi - ble, o - pen at page ___ one. ___ I thank

God he ___ stole the han - dle, and the train, ___ it won't ___ stop go-ing. No way to slow

Outro

Gtrs. 3 & 4: w/ Rhy. Figs. 1 & 1A (1st 2 meas., till fade)

Begin fade

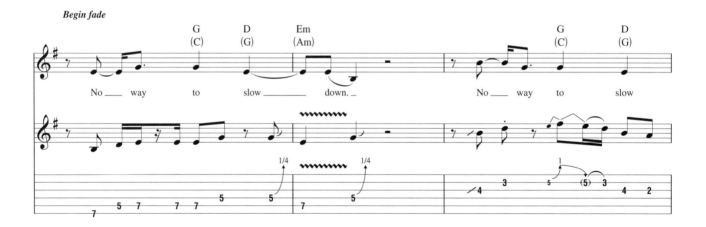

Fade out

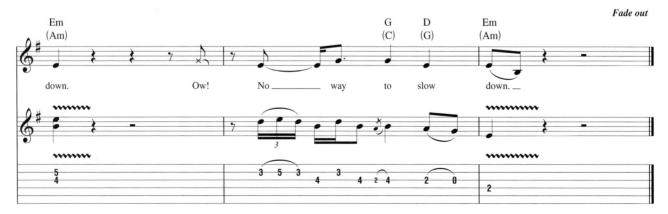

Lorelei

Words and Music by Dennis DeYoung and James Young

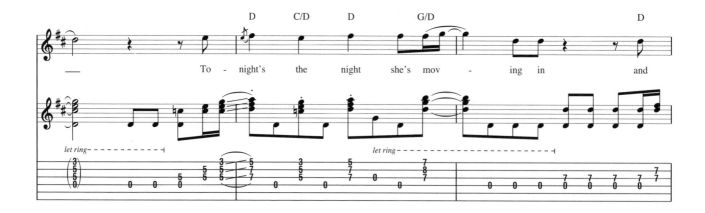

To - night's the night she's mov - ing in and

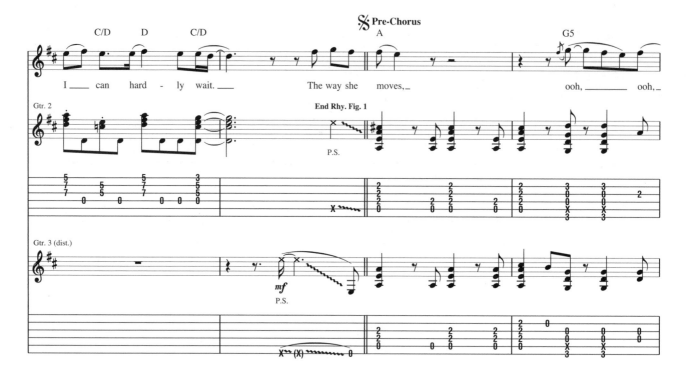

I can hard - ly wait. The way she moves, ooh, ooh,

Pre-Chorus

Gtr. 2

End Rhy. Fig. 1

Gtr. 3 (dist.)

mf

Chorus

I got - ta say, Lo - re - lei let's live to - geth -

let ring

216

Outro-Guitar Solo

Gtr. 5 tacet

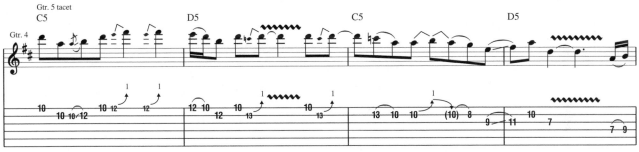

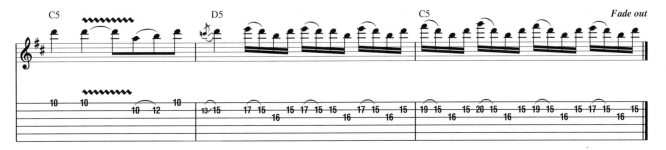

Magic Man

Words and Music by Ann Wilson and Nancy Wilson

try to un - der - stand. _____   Try _____ to un - der - stand. _____
try to un - der - stand. _____   Try _____ to un - der - stand. _____

End Rhy. Fig. 2

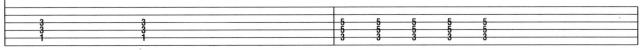

Try, try, ___ try ___ to un - der - stand: _____ I'm a mag - ic
Try, try, ___ try ___ to un - der - stand: _____ he's a mag - ic

End Rhy. Fig. 2A

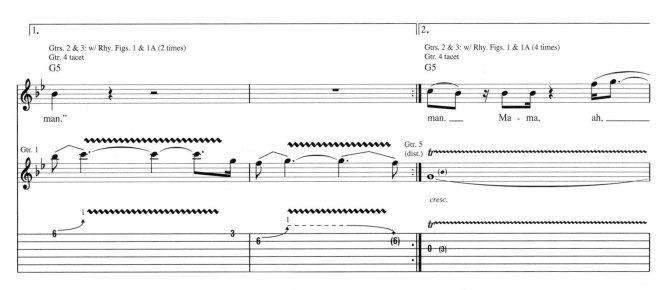

1.

Gtrs. 2 & 3: w/ Rhy. Figs. 1 & 1A (2 times)
Gtr. 4 tacet
G5

man."

Gtr. 1

2.

Gtrs. 2 & 3: w/ Rhy. Figs. 1 & 1A (4 times)
Gtr. 4 tacet
G5

man. ___ Ma - ma, ah,

Gtr. 5
(dist.)

cresc.

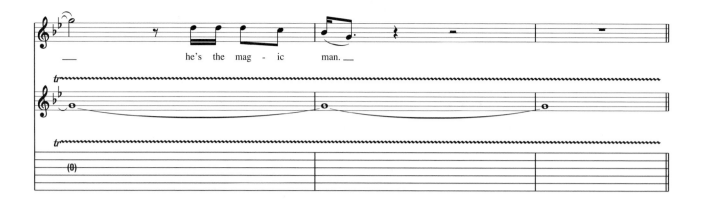

he's the mag - ic man. ___

Interlude

Gtrs. 1 & 2: w/ Rhy. Figs. 1 & 1A (4 times)

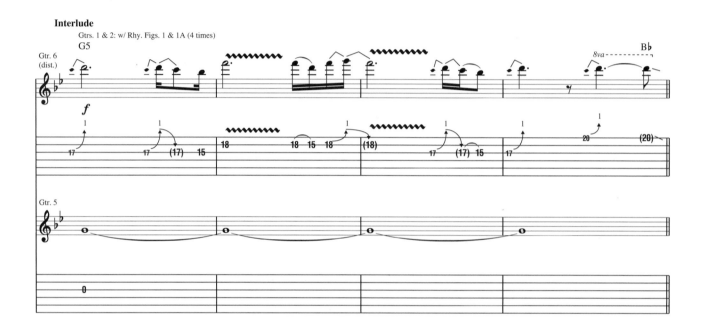

Chorus

Gtrs. 2 & 3: w/ Rhy. Fig. 2A (1st 6 meas.)
Gtr. 4: w/ Rhy. Fig. 2 (1st 6 meas.)
Gtrs. 5 & 6 tacet

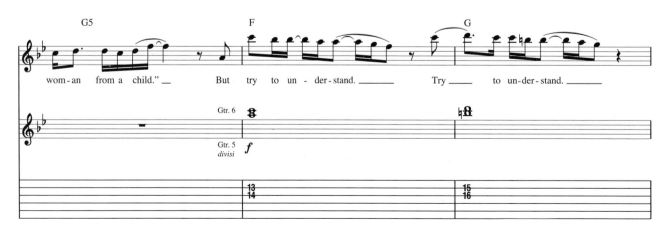

"Come on ___ home, _ girl," ___ he said with a smile. ___ "I cast my spell of love _ on you: a wom - an from a child." ___ But try to un - der - stand. _____ Try ___ to un-der- stand. _____

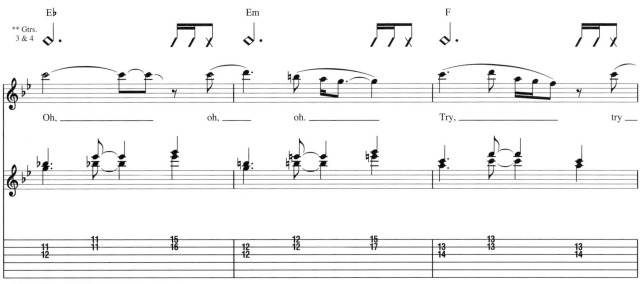

* Composite arrangement

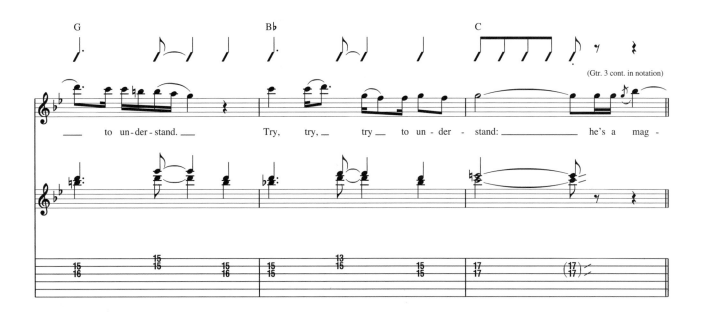

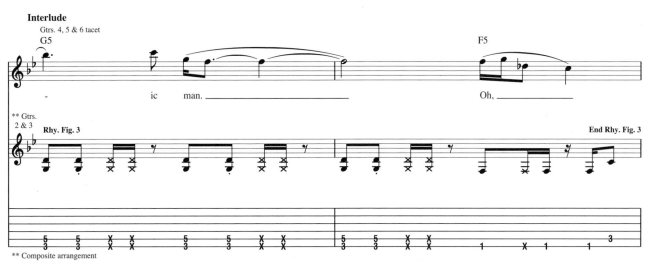

** Composite arrangement

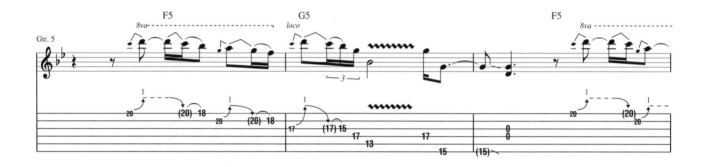

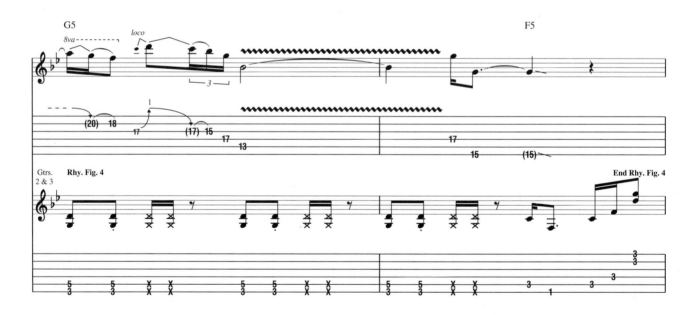

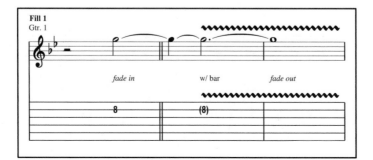

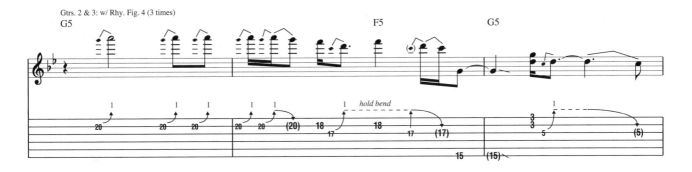

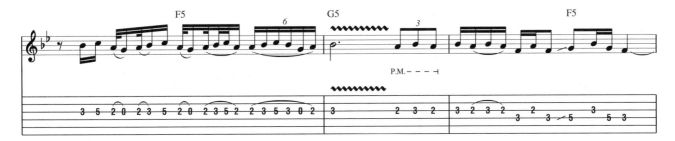

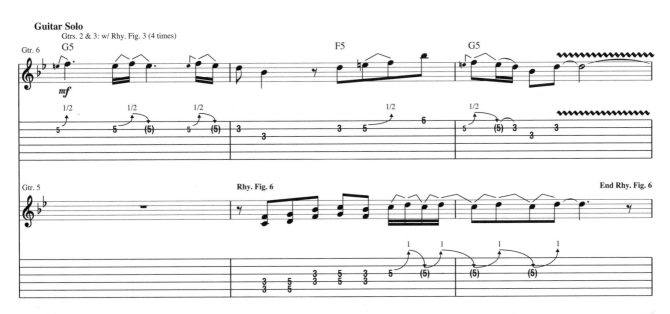

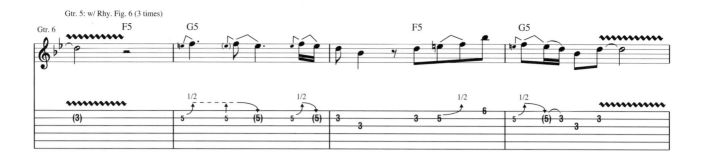

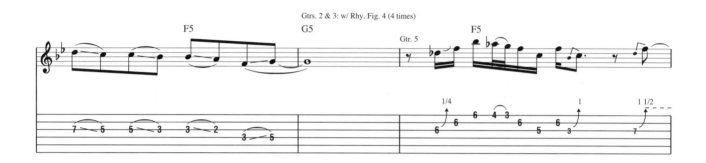

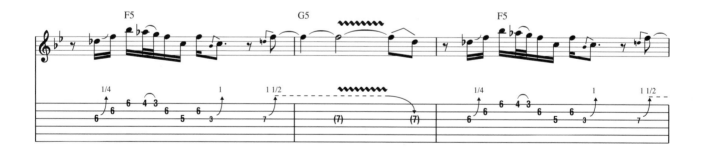

Chorus

"Come on ___ home, ___ girl," ___ he said with a smile. ___ "You don't have to love ___ me yet, let's ___

___ get high a - while." ___ But try to un - der - stand. _____ Try ___

___ to un - der - stand. _____ Try, try, ___ try ___ to un - der - stand: _____ he's a mag - ic

man, _____ yeah, _____ oh. _____

No Matter What

Written by Peter Ham

A5

*Chord symbols reflect implied harmony.

237

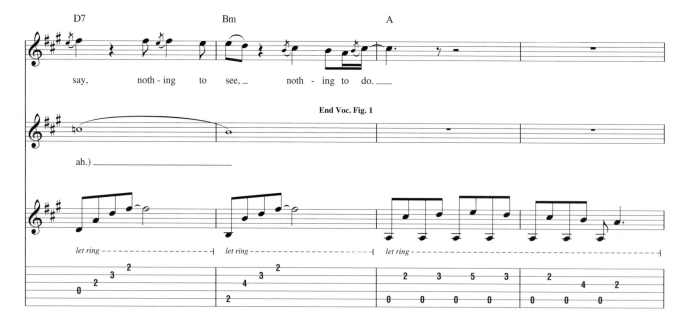

do, girl, ___ oo, girl, ___ with you? ___

Oo, girl, ___ you, girl, ___ want you. ___

*2nd time, upper note is D.

*2nd time, upper note is D.

Nobody's Fool

Words and Music by Tom Keifer

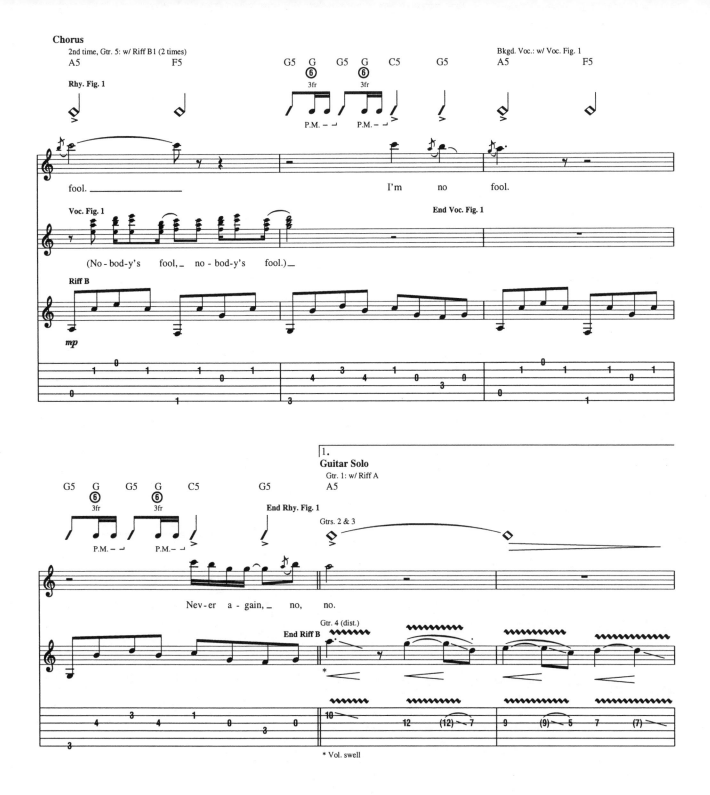

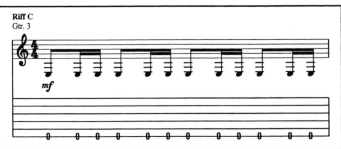

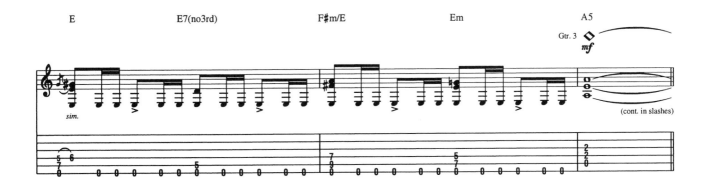

Guitar Solo

Gtr. 1: w/ Riff A (1 3/4 times)

Gtrs. 2 & 3: w/ Rhy. Fill 1

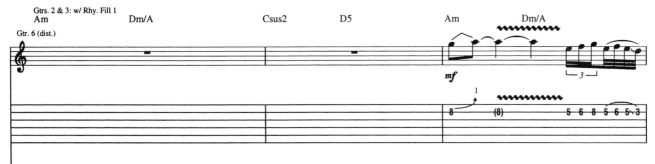

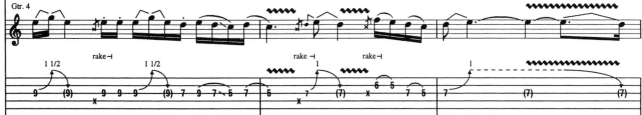

Gtr. 4 tacet

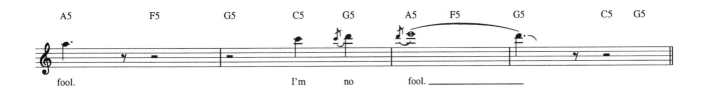

fool.   I'm   no   fool. _____

Outro Guitar Solo

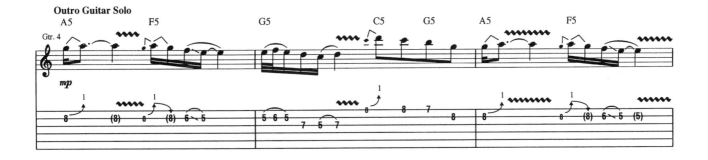

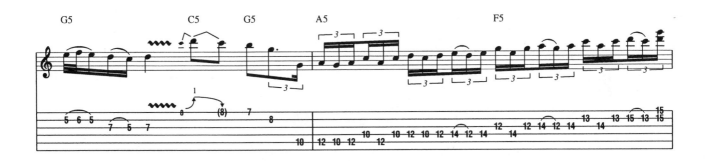

Begin fade

Bkgd. Voc.: w/ Voc. Fig. 1 (till fade)

Fade out

No, _____   no one loves a   fool. _____

Ramblin' Man

Words and Music by Dickey Betts

*Tune Up 1/2 Step:

①= E#   ④= D#
②= B#   ⑤= A#
③= G#   ⑥= E#

Intro

Fast Rock ♩ = 184

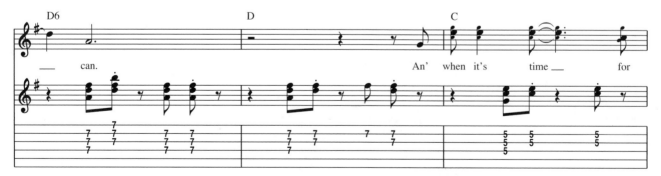

* or Capo I

* Gtr. 1 to left of slash in TAB.

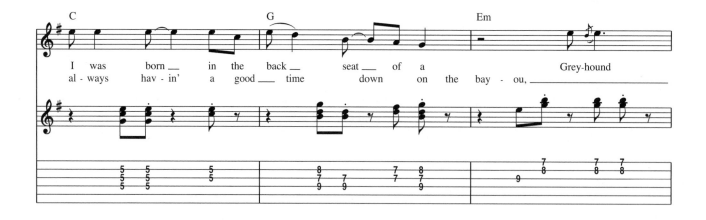

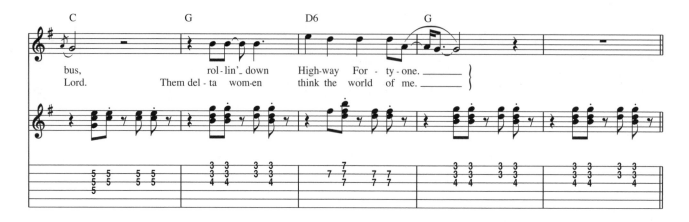

Chorus

Gtr. 1: w/Rhy. Fig. 1, simile

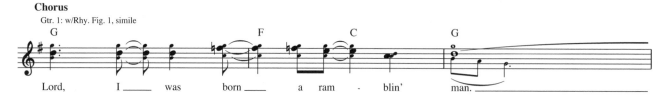

To Coda ⊕

250

Guitar Solo

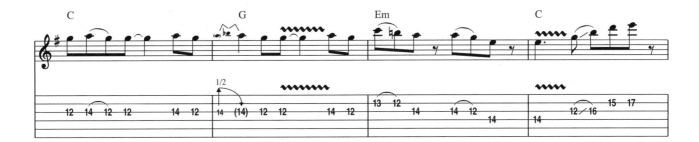

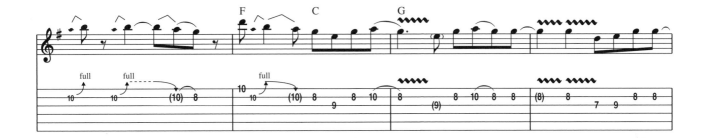

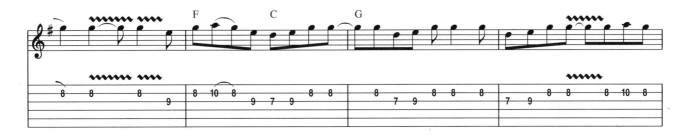

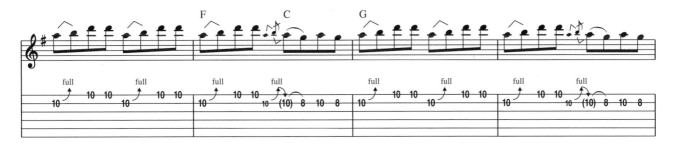

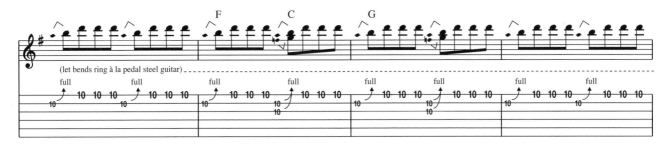

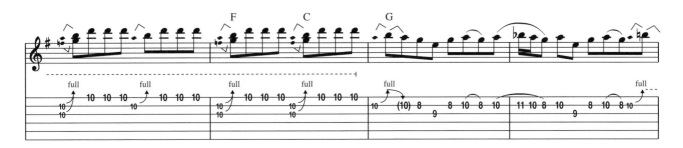

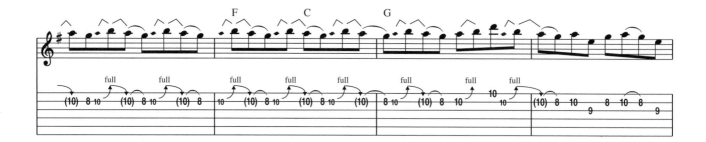

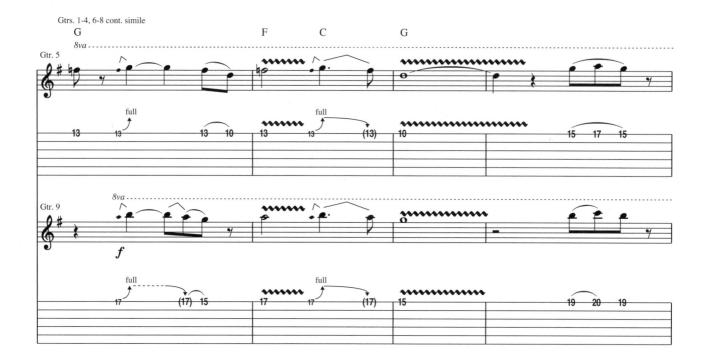

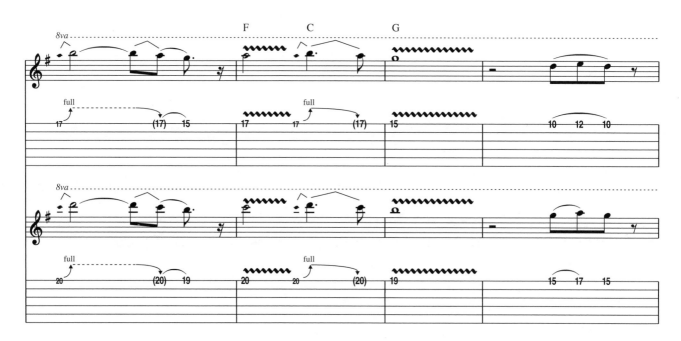

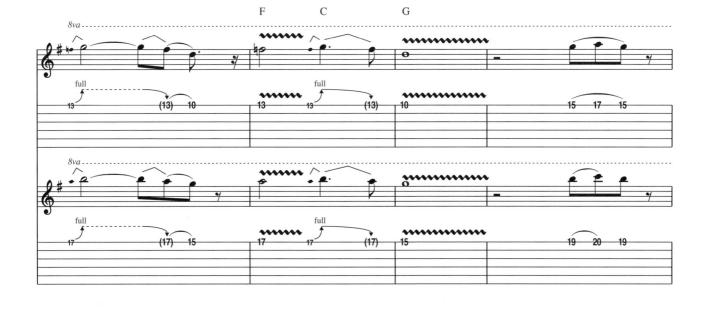

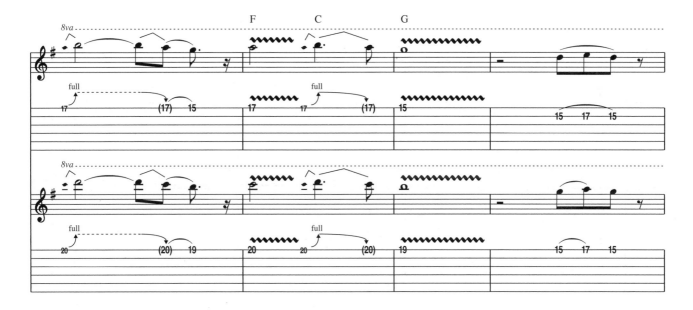

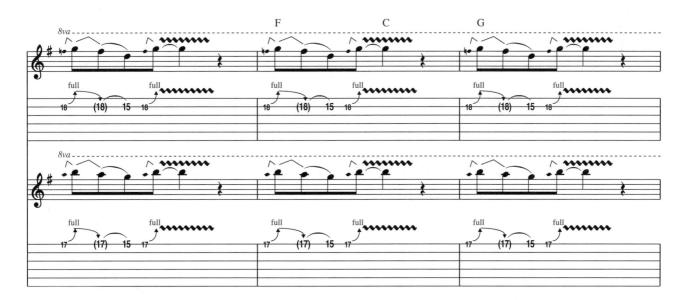

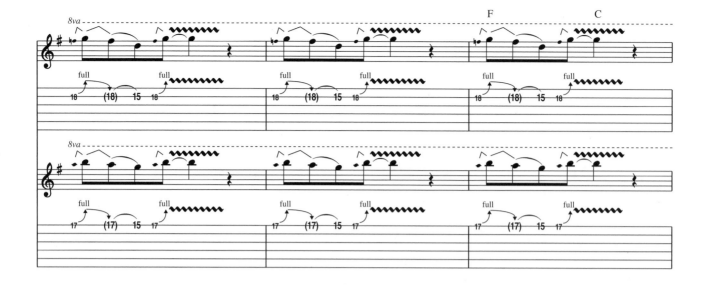

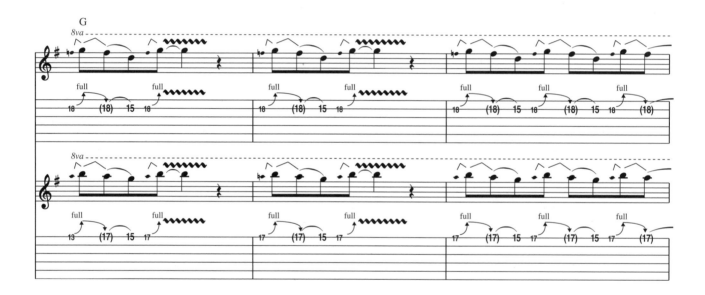

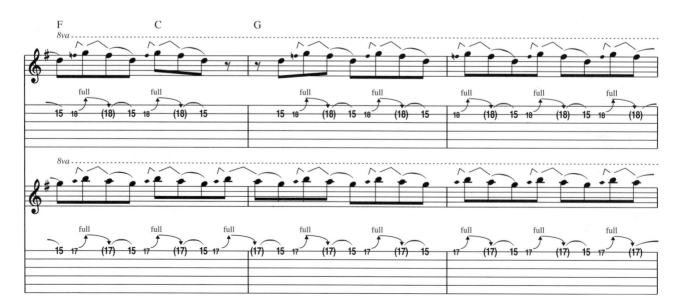

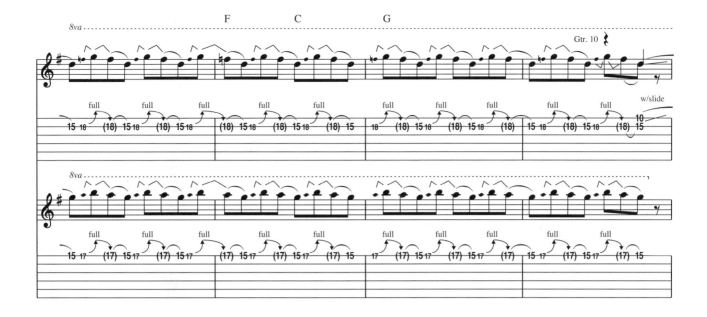

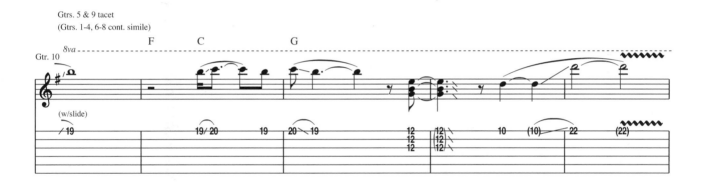

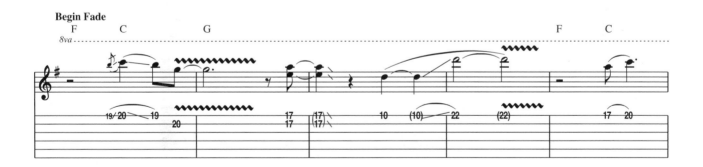

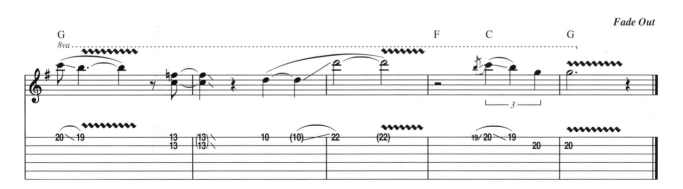

Rock & Roll Band

Words and Music by Tom Scholz

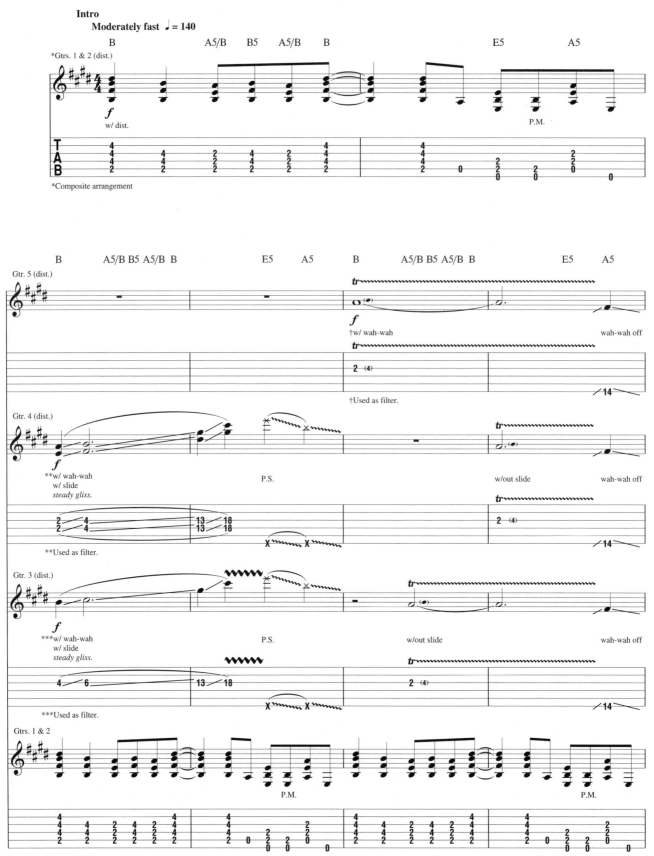

-ly made e-nough to sur-vive.____ But when we got up on stage____ and got read-
-ry 'bout the things we were miss - - ing. When we got____ up on stage____ and got read-

-y to play,___ peo-ple came___ a - live.___
-y to play,___ ev-'ry-bod-y'd lis - ten.

Gtrs. 3 & 4

Gtr. 5
divisi

Gtrs. 1 & 2

End Rhy. Fig. 1

Chorus

Gtrs. 3, 4 & 5 tacet

C#m   A5   B5   C#m/G#

Rock and roll band,___ ev-'ry-bod-y's wait - in', get-tin' cra - zy, an-

Fill 1   End Fill 1

Gtrs. 3, 4 & 5

Gtrs. 1 & 2

let ring   *let ring*   *let ring*

Guitar Solo

3. Play -

Verse

Gtrs. 1 & 2: w/ Rhy. Fig. 1

-in' for a week in Rhode Is - land,   a man ___ came to the stage one ___ night. ___

Gtrs. 3, 4 & 5

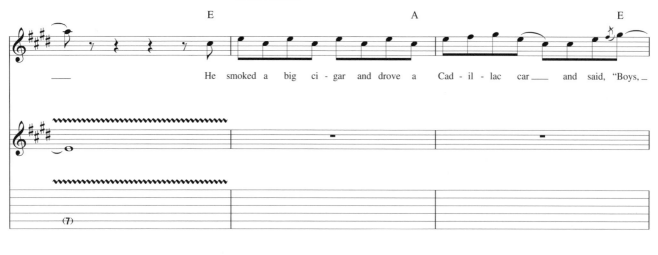

He smoked a big ci - gar and drove a Cad - il - lac car ___ and said, "Boys, ___

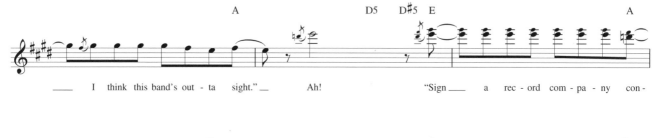

___ I think this band's out - ta sight." ___ Ah! "Sign ___ a rec - ord com - pa - ny con -

- tract, you know ___ I've got great ex - pec - ta - tions. When I hear ___

___ you on the car ra - di - o ___ you're gon - na be a sen - sa - tion." ___ Yeah, ___

Chorus

Gtrs. 3, 4 & 5: w/ Fill 1

___ yeah. ___ Rock and roll band, ___ ev - 'ry - bod - y's wait - in',

264

265

Run to You

Words and Music by Bryan Adams and Jim Vallance

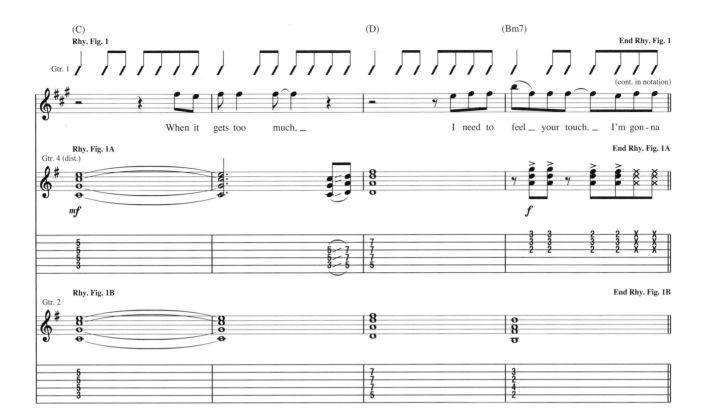

When it gets too much, — I need to feel — your touch. I'm gon-na

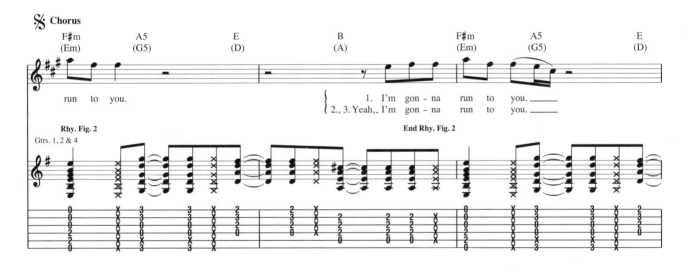

𝄋 Chorus

| F♯m | A5 | E | B | F♯m | A5 | E |
| (Em) | (G5) | (D) | (A) | (Em) | (G5) | (D) |

run to you.

1. I'm gon-na run to you. _____
2., 3. Yeah,_ I'm gon-na run to you. _____

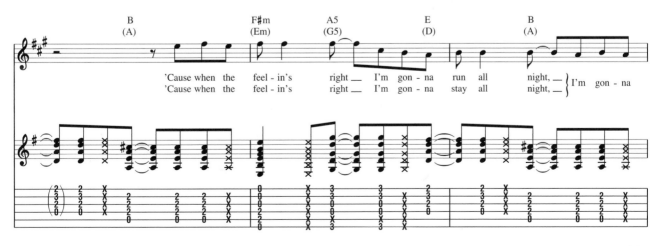

| B | F♯m | A5 | E | B |
| (A) | (Em) | (G5) | (D) | (A) |

'Cause when the feel-in's right _ I'm gon-na run all night, _ I'm gon-na
'Cause when the feel-in's right _ I'm gon-na stay all night, _

Smokin' in the Boys Room

Words and Music by Michael Koda and Michael Lutz

know it's my cue. ___ I'm gon - na meet the boys on floor num - ber two.

Mick and Tom, to get caught would sure - ly be the death of us all.

𝄋 Chorus

2nd time, Gtr. 2: w/ Fill 1

Smok-in' in the boy's room.

Smok-in' in the boy's room.

Now, teach-

Gtr. 2 (dist.)

Gtr. 1

Rhy. Fig. 1

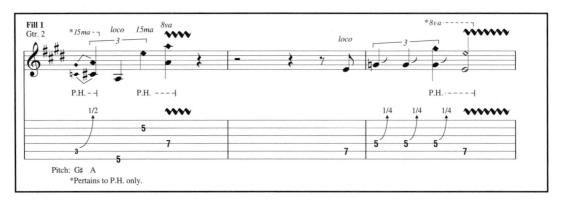

Fill 1
Gtr. 2

Pitch: G♯ A
*Pertains to P.H. only.

274

Guitar Solo

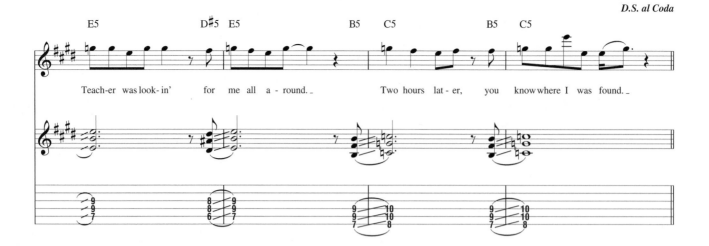

E5   D#5 E5   B5 C5   B5 C5

Teach-er was look-in' for me all a - round. _ Two hours lat - er, you know where I was found. _

Coda

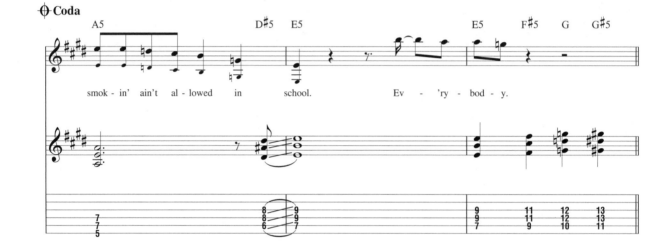

A5   D#5 E5   E5 F#5 G G#5

smok - in' ain't al - lowed in school. Ev - 'ry - bod - y.

1.   2.

Interlude

Gtr. 1 tacet

N.C.

Smok - in' in the boy's room.   Smok - in' in the boy's room. I tell _ you, I was _ Hey, teach-

(Oo.)

*1st time only.

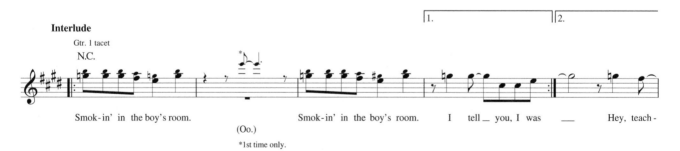

B5 B6   B5 B6 B5 A5   A6   A5   A6 A5 B5   B6   B5 B6

- er, don't ya fill me up with your rule, _ 'cause ev - 'ry - bod - y knows that

Gtr. 1

P.M. -

Space Truckin'

Words and Music by Ritchie Blackmore, Ian Gillan, Roger Glover, Jon Lord and Ian Paice

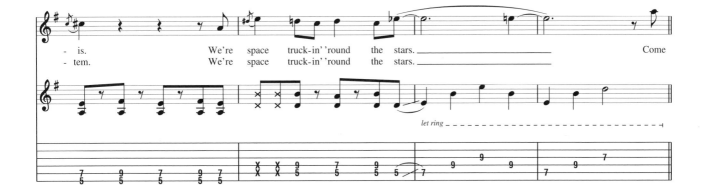

- is. We're space truck-in' 'round the stars. _____ Come
- tem. We're space truck-in' 'round the stars. _____

let ring _

𝄋 Chorus

N.C.(A5)

on! Come on! Come on! Let's go space truck-in'. Come

Riff A

To Coda 1 ⊕
To Coda 2 ⊕

(E5)   (F5) (F♯5) (G5)

on! Come on! Come on! Space truck-in'. { 2. Re -
                                        { The

End Riff A

Bridge

Am   C5   D5

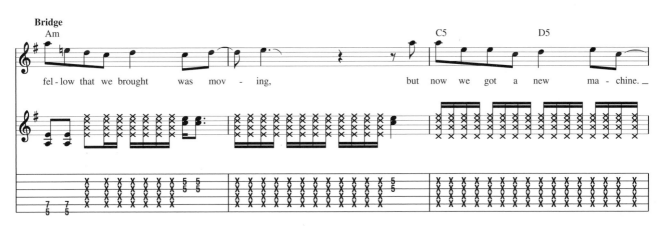

fel - low that we brought was mov - ing, but now we got a new ma - chine. _

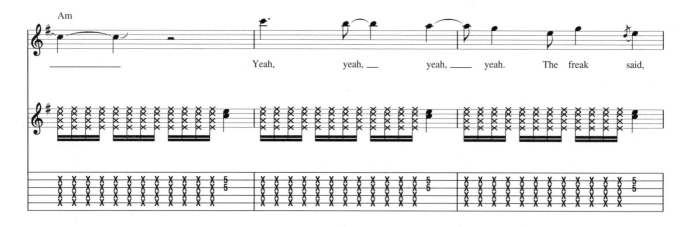

Yeah, yeah, yeah, yeah. The freak said,

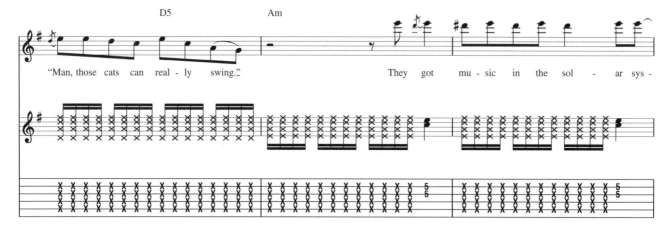

"Man, those cats can real-ly swing." They got mu-sic in the sol - ar sys -

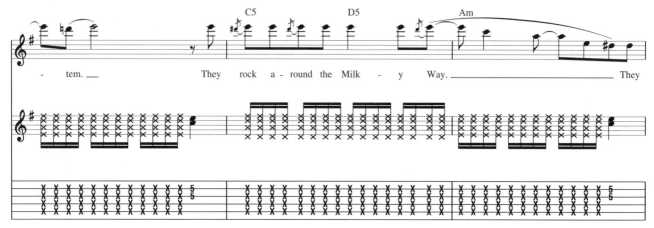

- tem. They rock a-round the Milk - y Way. They

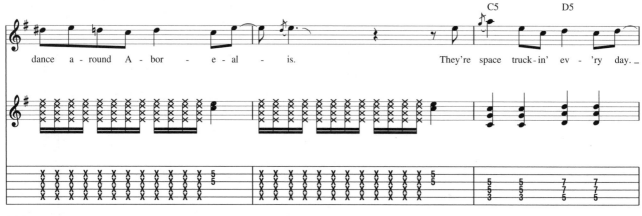

dance a-round A - bor - e - al - is. They're space truck-in' ev - 'ry day.

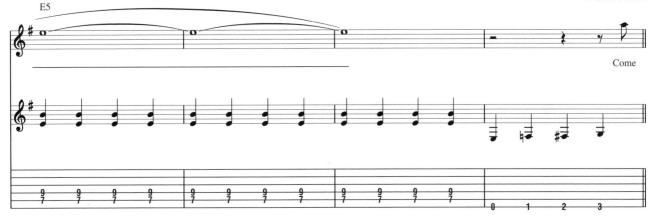

Come

Coda 1

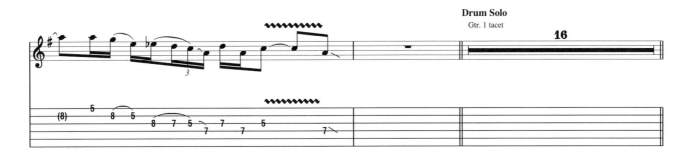

Thirty Days in the Hole

Words and Music by Steve Marriott

*Symbols in parentheses represent chord names respective to capoed guitar.
Symbols above reflect actual sounding chords. Capoed fret is "0" in tab.

285

Too Hot to Handle

Words and Music by Phil Moog and Pete Way

1. Caught in the cross-fire, a warn-in' fight, ___ leg-ends make or break game.

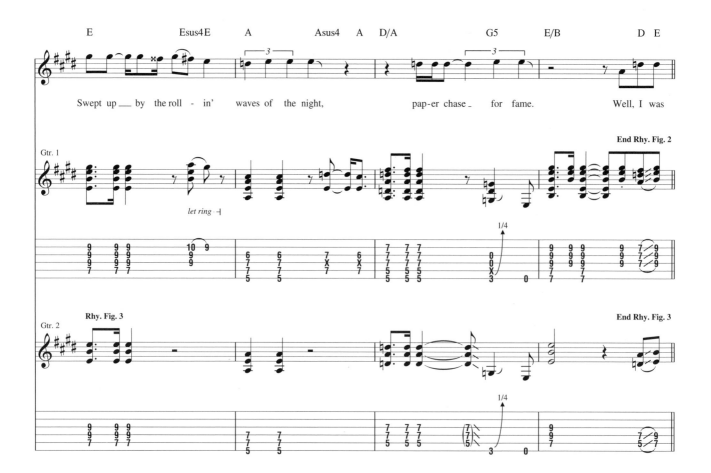

Swept up __ by the roll - in' waves of the night, pap-er chase __ for fame. Well, I was

Chorus

too, _____ too hot, ba - by, ___ too hot __ to han - dle. Yeah, I was

293

Coda 1

D.S.S. al Coda 2

Coda 2

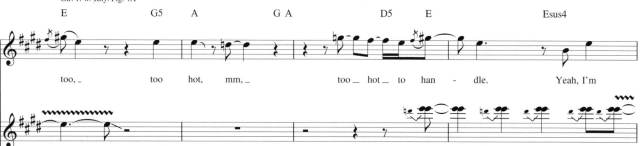

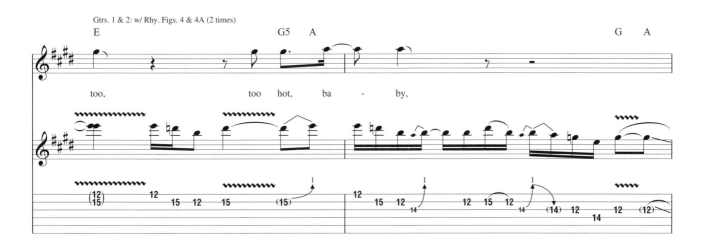

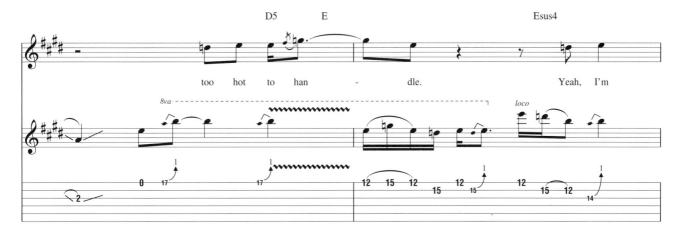

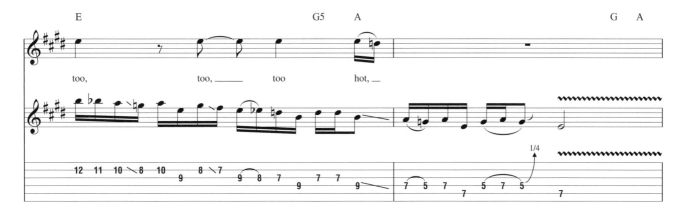

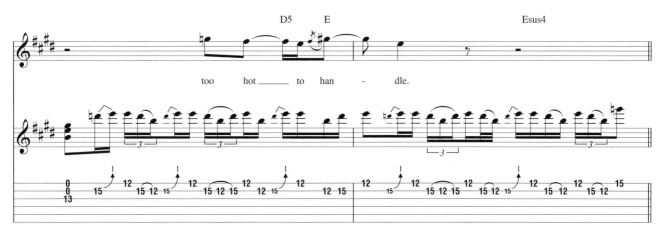

Outro-Guitar Solo

Gtrs. 1 & 2: w/ Rhy. Figs. 4 & 4A (1 1/2 times)

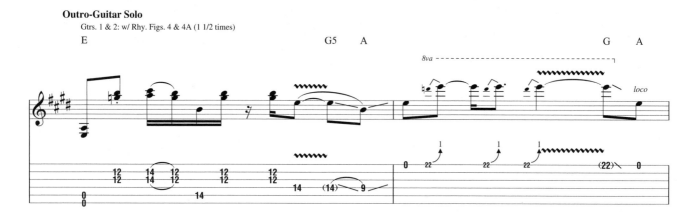

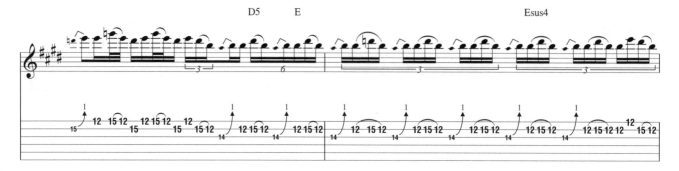

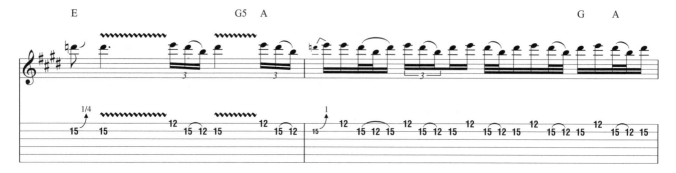

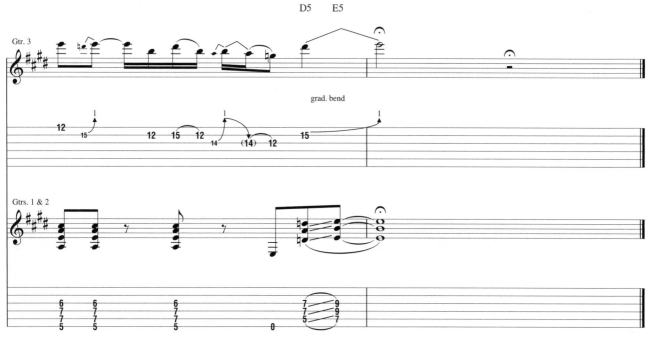

Too Late for Love

Words and Music by Joe Elliott, Richard Savage, Richard Allen, Steve Clark, Peter Willis and R.J. Lange

Too late, it's too late,

too late, too late, too late.

Interlude

(Oh. Oh. Oh.

Oh. It's a lit-tle too late, Oh. much too

late. Oh. Can you see it's all too

Oh.)

late?

Yeah! _____ It's too late. _

Turn to Stone

Words and Music by Joe Walsh and Terry Trebandt

it's get-tin' strong - er. I don't think they can last _ much long-er. _ Turn _ to stone. _

* Chord symbols reflect overall tonality.

backyard peo-ple and they worked all day. The day gets wast-ed, safe to say _ they're tast - in'. _ Make the words _

_ rhyme. _ And you know _ it's get-tin' strong-er. I can't make _ 'em run that much long-er. Turn _ to

Chorus

stone. _

Interlude

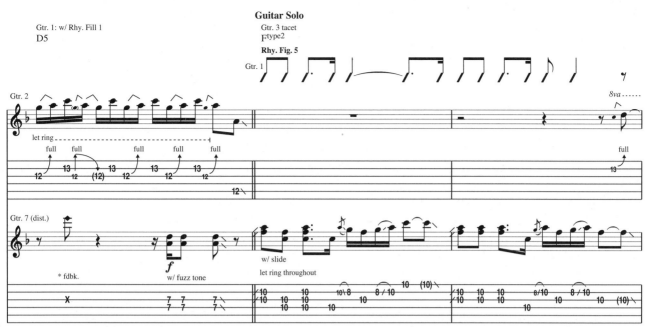

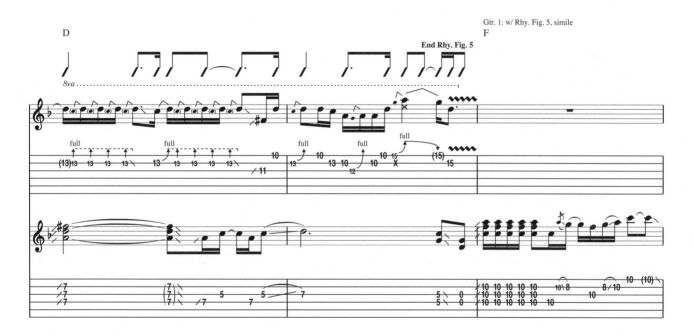

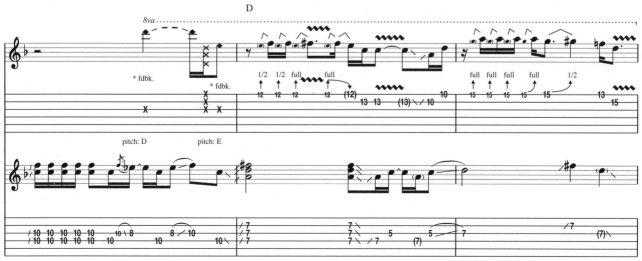

* Microphone fdbk., not caused by string vibration.

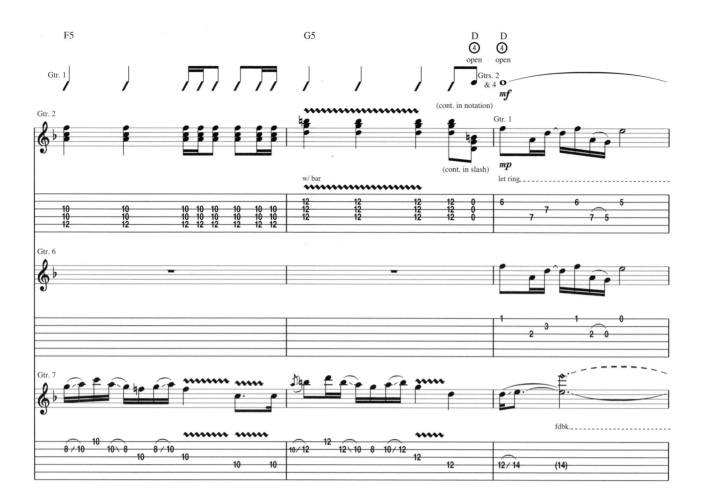

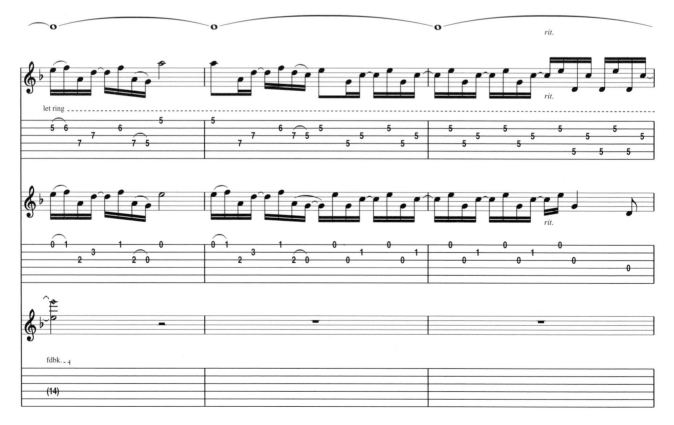

Free Time

A Tempo

Gtr. 6 tacet

Gtrs. 2, 4 & 7 tacet

w/ bar
let ring

Gtr. 1

slack
* Pull up and down w/ vibrato bar randomly, approx. 4 seconds.

Gtr. 1: w/ Rhy. Fig. 4, 2 times, simile

Gtr. 5: w/ Fill 1

Gtr. 4

Outro

Gtrs. 4 & 5

1 1/2   1 1/2

Fill 1
Gtr. 5

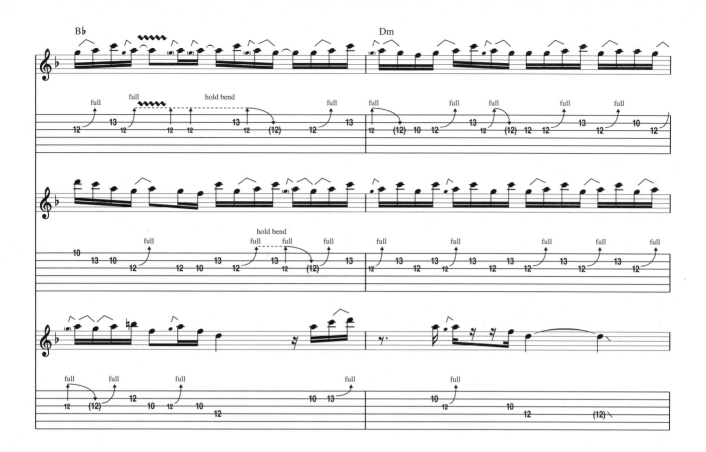

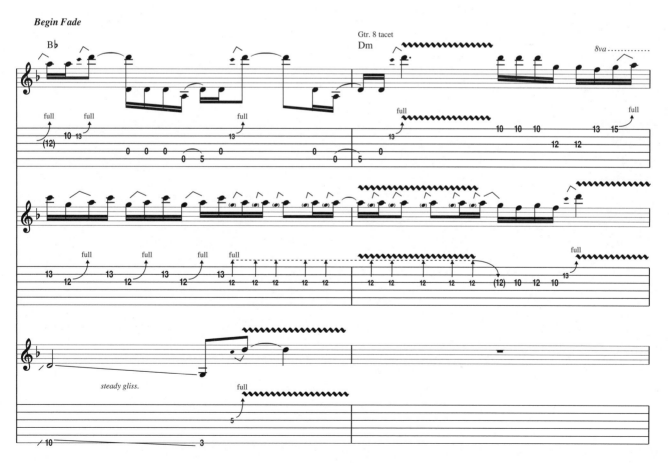

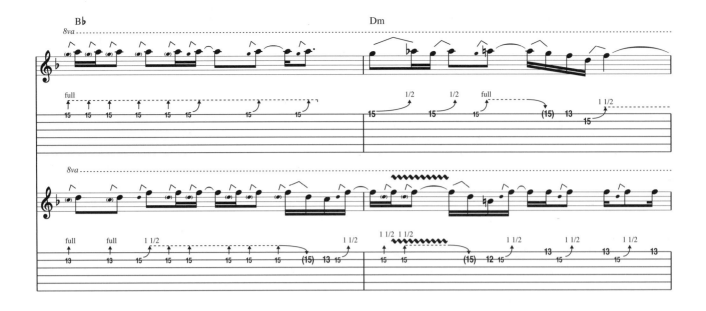

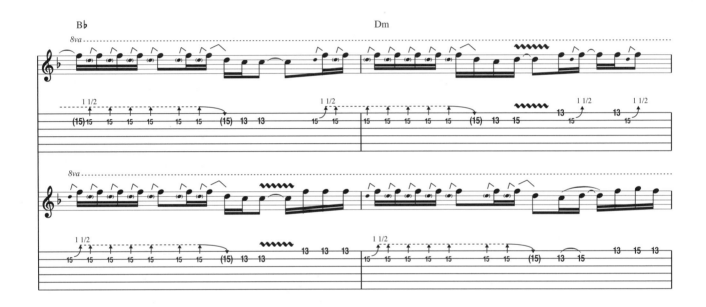

Fade Out

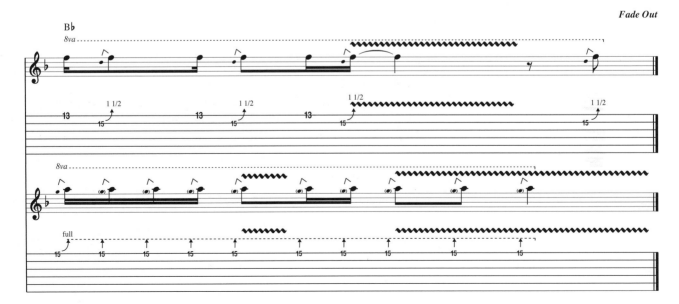

(You Can Still) Rock in America

Words and Music by Jack Blades and Brad Gillis

*Chord symbols reflect implied harmony

**Bass plays E.

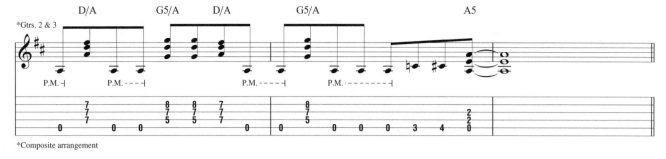

*Composite arrangement

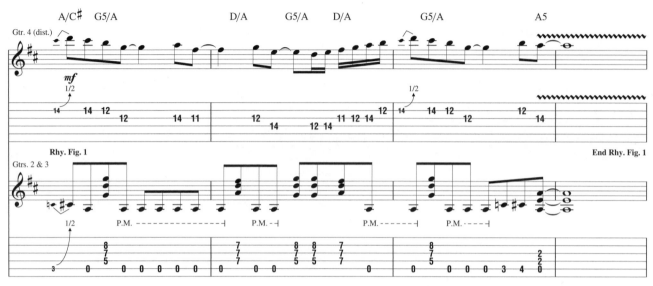

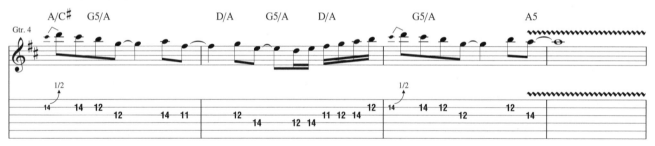

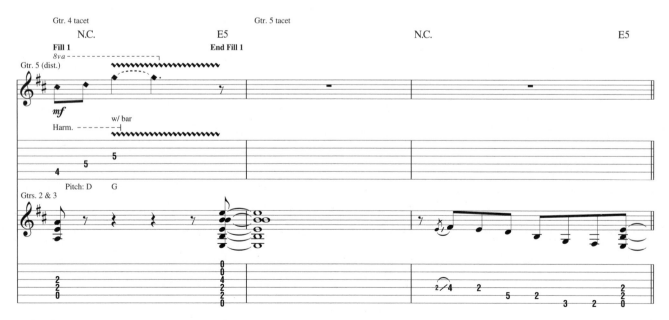

2nd time, Gtr. 2: w/ Rhy. Fill 1

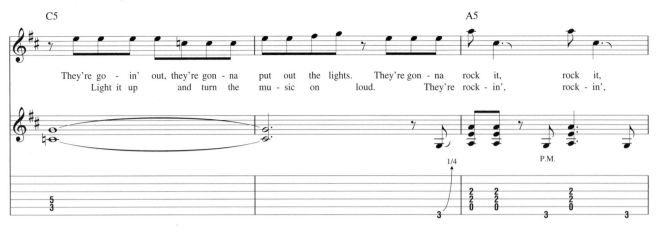

They're go - in' out, they're gon - na   put out the lights. They're gon - na   rock it,   rock it,
Light it up   and turn the   mu - sic on   loud. They're rock - in',   rock - in',

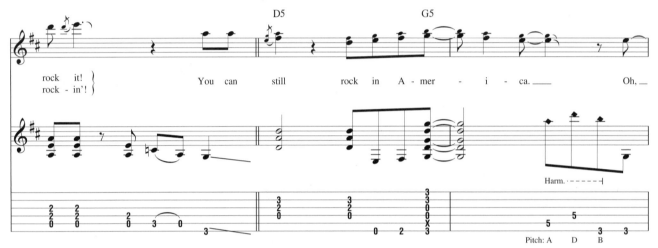

𝄋 **Chorus**

rock   it! }
rock - in'! }
You can   still   rock in A - mer - i - ca. ___   Oh, ___

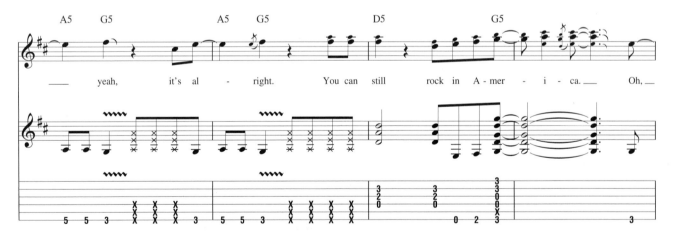

___   yeah,   it's al - right.   You can still   rock in A - mer - i - ca. ___   Oh, ___

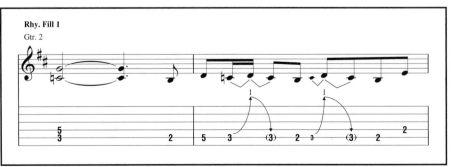

Rhy. Fill 1

Gtr. 2

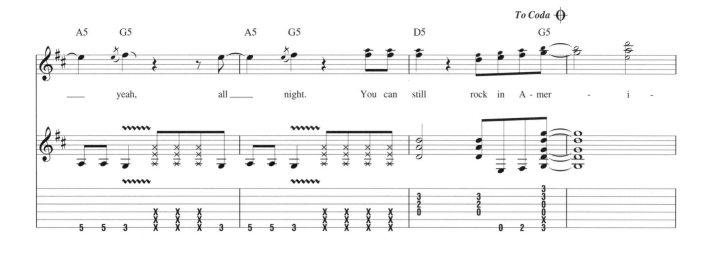

yeah,   all ___ night.   You can still   rock in A - mer   -   i -

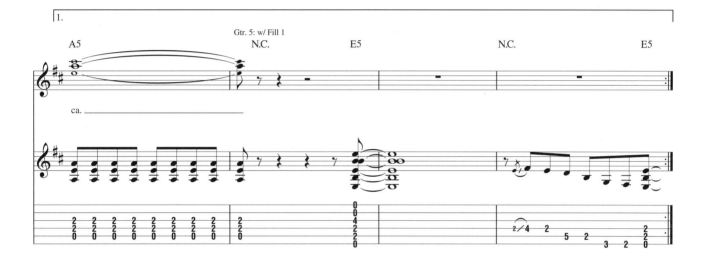

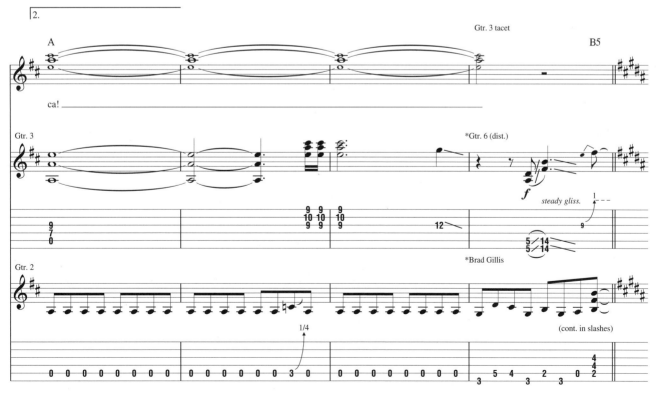

Guitar Solo

Half-time feel

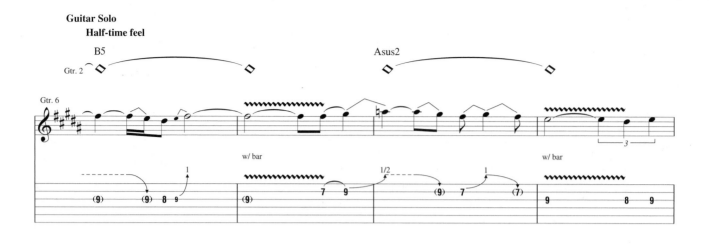

End half-time feel

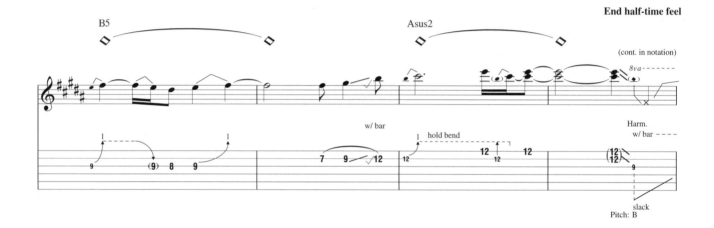

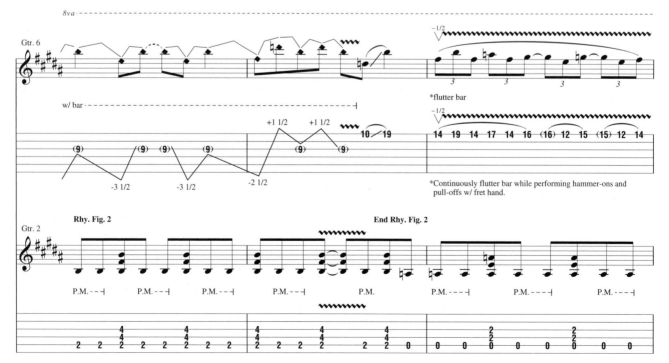

*Tap sequence executed with designated fingers
(1 = index, 2 = middle, 3 = ring, 4 = pinky) of pick hand, next 8 meas.

**Pluck open string w/ fret hand index finger.

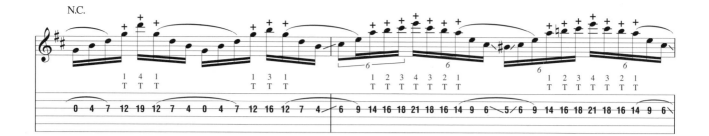

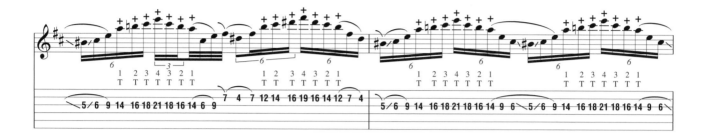

Bridge

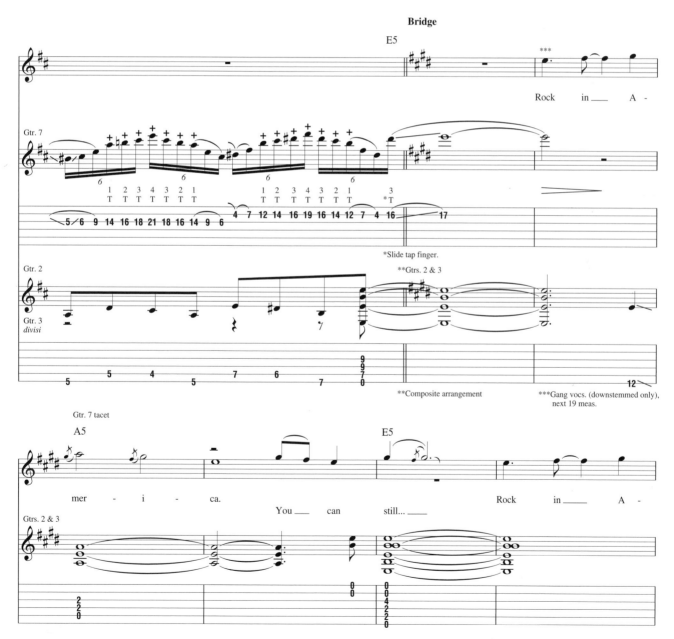

Guitar Solo

Gtrs. 2 & 3: w/ Rhy. Fig. 2

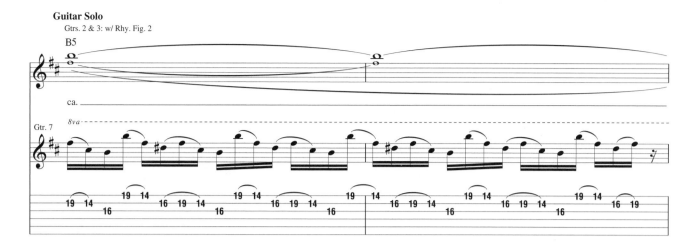

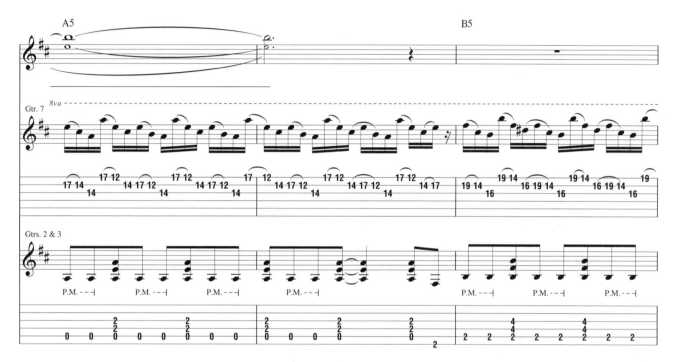

D.S. al Coda

Gtr. 7 tacet

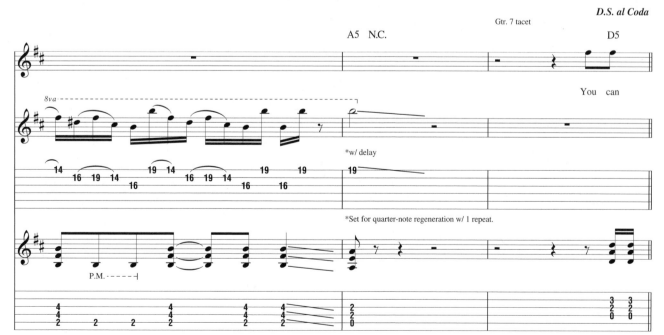

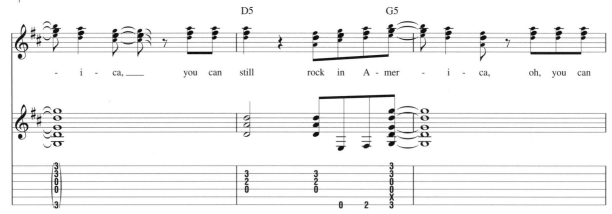

D5   G5

-i - ca, ___ you can still rock in A - mer - i - ca, oh, you can

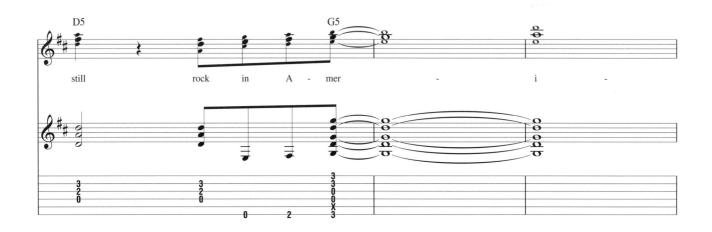

D5   G5

still rock in A - mer - i -

Gtr. 2: w/ Rhy. Fig. 1 (3 times)

A/C#   G5/A   D/A   G5/A   D/A   G5/A   A5

ca. _____

Gtr. 4

Gtr. 3

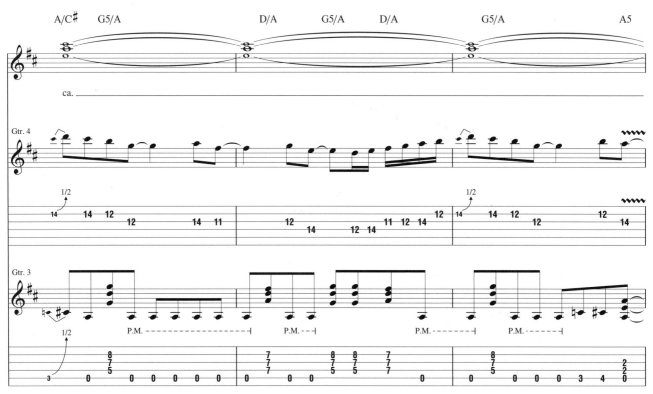

You Make Lovin' Fun

Words and Music by Christine McVie

***Symbols in parentheses represent chord names respective to tuned down guitars.
Symbols above reflect actual sounding chords. Chord symbols reflect overall harmony.

You make me hap-py with the things __ you do. ___ Oh, __

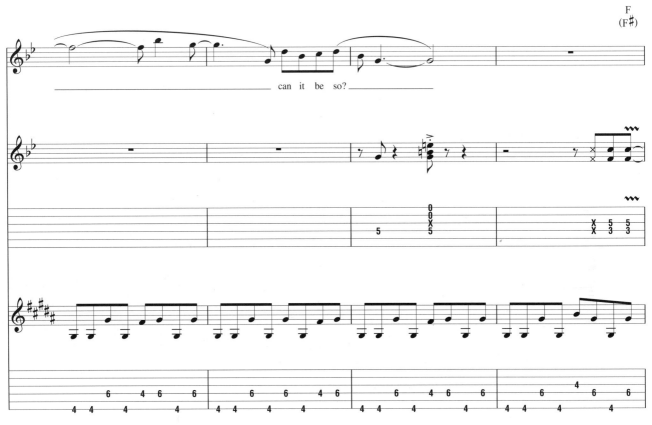

can it be so? ___

This feel - ing fol - lows me wher - ev - er I go. ___

Gtr. 1

Gtr. 2

Rhy. Fill 1   End Rhy. Fill 1

Gtr. 3

End Riff A

Chorus
Half-time feel

Gtr. 2 tacet   Gtr. 3 tacet
(B)   (B/A)

Rhy. Fig. 2

**Gtr. 4   ***Voc. Fig. 1

mf

I nev - er did be - lieve ___ in ___ mir - a - cles, ___
Male & Female: (Ah.) ___

*Gtrs. 1 & 5

w/ chorus
let ring - - - - - -

*Gtr. 5 (clean) w/ chorus & reverb, played *mf*

Gtr. 3

**Organ arr. for gtr.   ***Applies to Bkgd. Voc. only.

Guitar Solo

Gtr. 2: w/ Rhy. Fig. 1 (1 7/8 times) Gtr. 5 tacet
Gtr. 3 w/ Riff A

D.S. al Coda

Gtr. 2: w/ Rhy. Fill 1

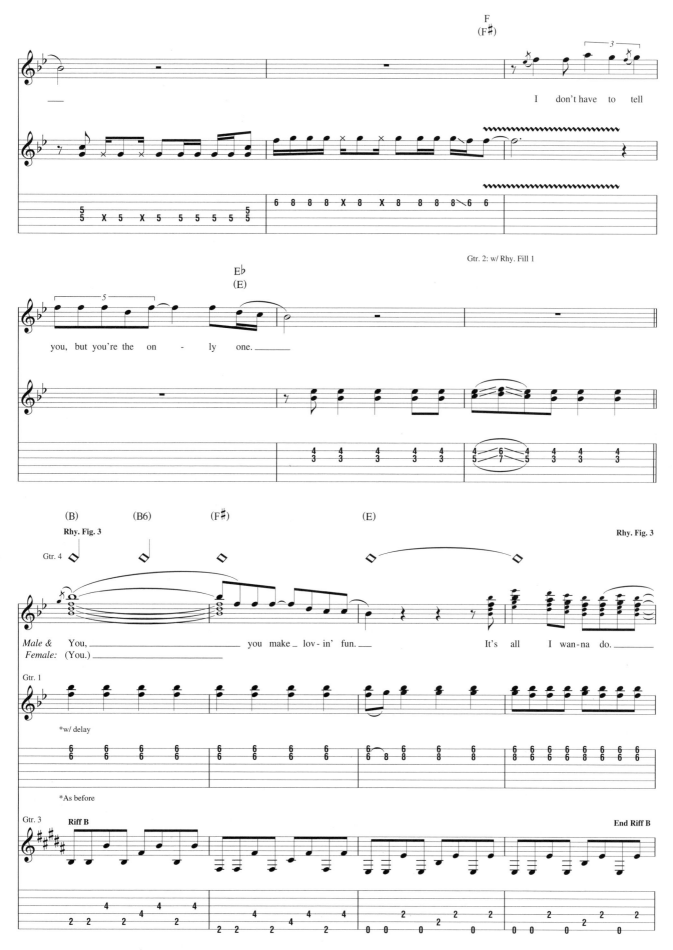

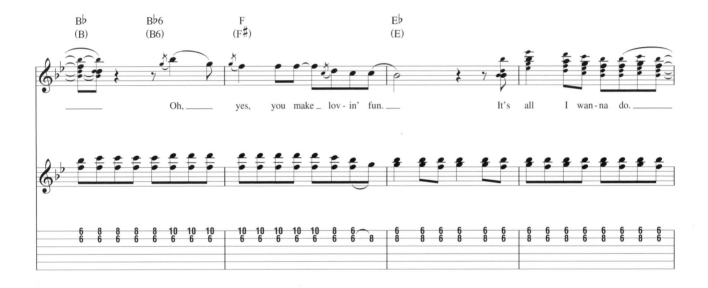

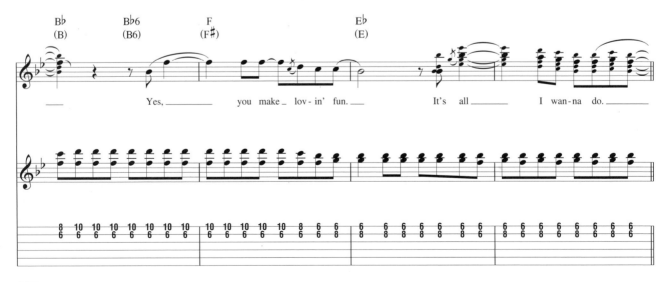

Outro

Gtr. 3: w/ Riff B (2 times)
Gtr. 4: w/ Rhy. Fig. 3 (2 times)

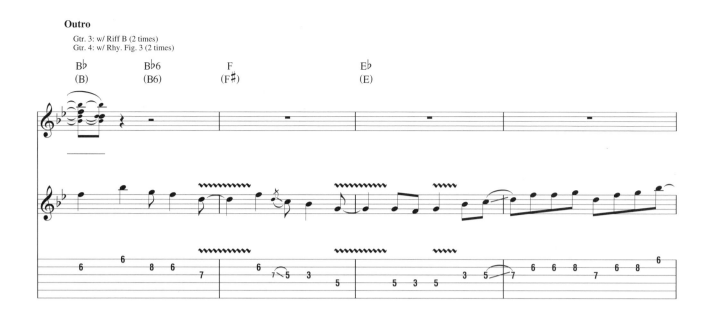

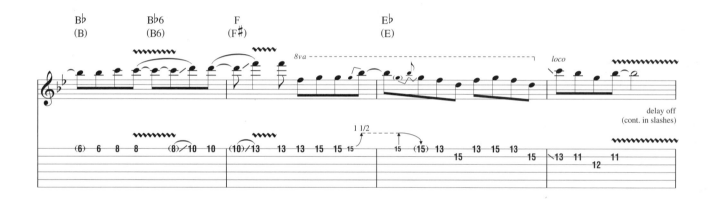

The Zoo

Words and Music by Rudolf Schenker and Klaus Meine

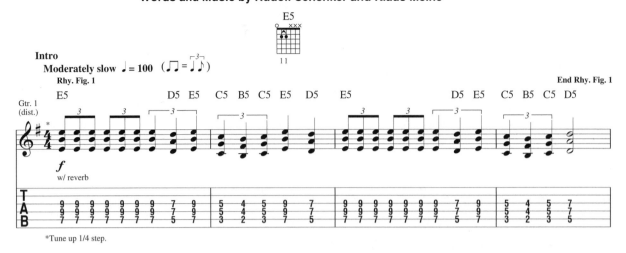

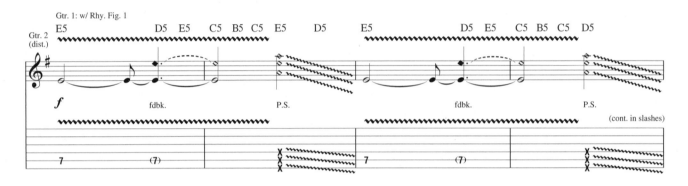

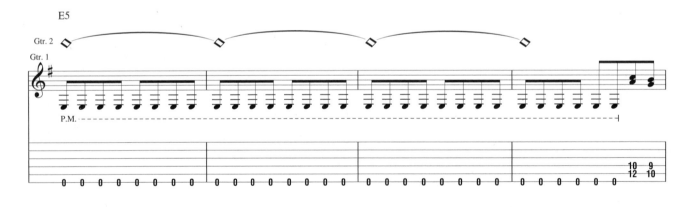

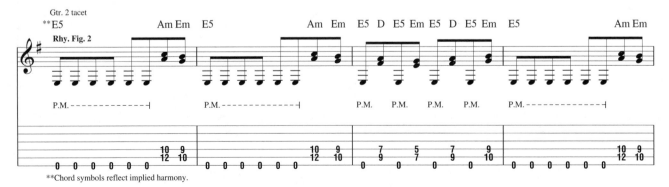

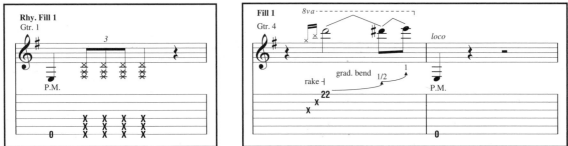

hun-gry eyes _ are pass-ing by _ on streets we call The Zoo. _ We

eat the night, _ we drink the time, _ make our dreams _ come true. _ And

eat the night,___ we drink the time,___ make our dreams___ come true.___

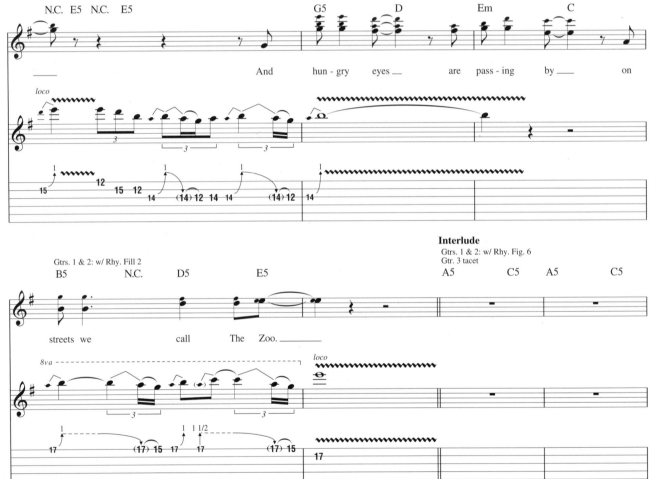

___ And hun-gry eyes ___ are pass-ing by ___ on

Interlude
Gtrs. 1 & 2: w/ Rhy. Fig. 6
Gtr. 3 tacet

streets we call The Zoo.___

Outro - Guitar Solo
Gtr. 1: w/ Rhy. Fig. 2 (1st meas.)
Gtr. 1: w/ Rhy. Fig. 2 (till fade)

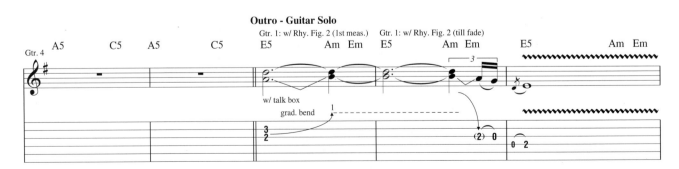

w/ talk box
grad. bend

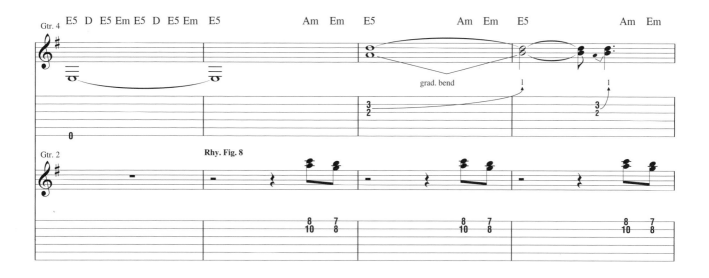

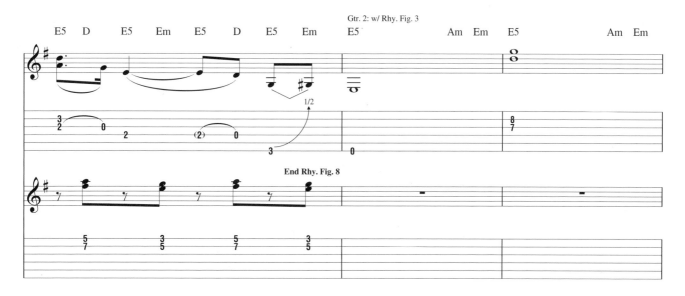

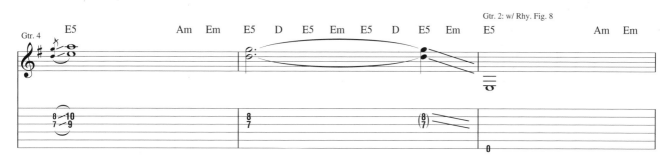

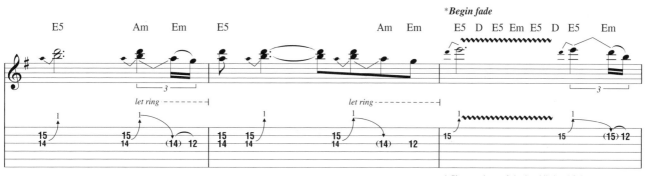

* City soundscape fades in while band fades out.

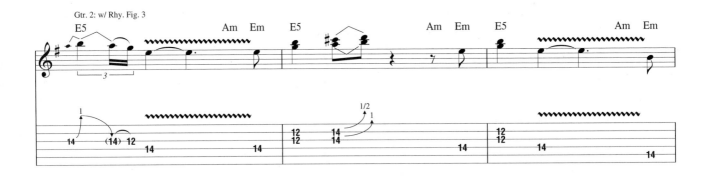

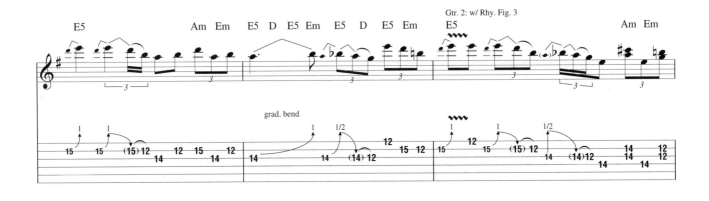

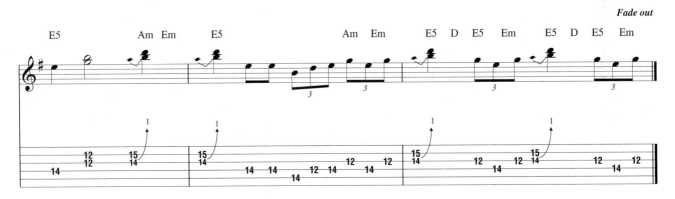